ANARCHISM AND SOCIALISM • PLEKHANOV, GEORGII VALENTINOVICH

Publishers' Note 7 1

Preface 13 2

I. The Point of View of the Utopian Socialists 17 3

II. The Point of View of Scientific Socialism 30 6

III. The Historical Development of the Anarchist Doctrine 38 8

IV. Proudhon 53 11

V. Bakounine 78 17

VI. Bakounine —(Concluded) 89 ... 20

VII. The Smaller Fry 103 23

VIII. The So-called Anarchist Tactics. Their Morality 127 29

IX. The Bourgeoisie, Anarchism, and Socialism 143 33

Publisher's Note
Purchase of this book entitles you to a free trial membership in the publisher's book club at www.rarebooksclub.com. (Time limited offer.) Simply enter the barcode number from the back cover onto the membership form on our home page. The book club entitles you to select from millions of books at no additional charge. You can also download a digital copy of this and related books to read on the go. Simply enter the title or subject onto the search form to find them.
Note: This is an historic book. Pages numbers, where present in the text, refer to the first edition of the book and may also be in indexes.
If you have any questions, could you please be so kind as to consult our Frequently Asked Questions page at www.rarebooksclub.com/faqs.cfm? You are also welcome to contact us there.
Publisher: Books LLC™, Memphis, TN, USA, 2012. ISBN: 9781153826907.
Proofreading: pgdp.net

⁂ ⁂ ⁂ ⁂ ⁂ ⁂ ⁂ ⁂

Transcriber's Note:

Obvious typographical errors have been corrected.
An image of the Front cover can be seen here 0
, and of the back cover
here 0
.
Images of the original pages can be seen by clicking on the page numbers in the right margin.
[1]

ANARCHISM AND SOCIALISM
[2]
[3]
ANARCHISM
AND
SOCIALISM
BY
GEORGE PLECHANOFF
Translated with the permission of the author by
ELEANOR MARX AVELING
CHICAGO
CHARLES H. KERR & COMPANY
[4]

[5]
[6]
[7]

PUBLISHERS' NOTE

In reprinting *Anarchism and Socialism*, by George Plechanoff, we realize that there is not the same need for assailing and exposing anarchism at present as there has been at different times in the past. Yet the book is valuable, not merely because of its historic interest but also to workers coming into contact with the revolutionary movement for the first time. The general conception of anarchism that a beginner often gets is that it is something extremely advanced. It is often expressed somewhat as follows: "After capitalism comes socialism and then comes anarchism." Plechanoff very ably explodes such notions.

Within the pages of this work the author shows not only the reactionary character of anarchism, but he exposes its class bias and its empty philosophic idealism and utopian program. He shows anarchism to be just the opposite of scientific socialism or communism. It aims at a society dominated by individualism, which is simply a capitalist ideal. Such ideals as "liberty," "equality," "fraternity," first sprang from the ranks of the petty property owners of early capitalism, as Plechanoff shows. He also points out that while Proudhon [8] is usually credited with being "the father of anarchism" that actually Max Stirner comes closer to being its "father." Stirner's "League of Egoists," he says, "is only the utopia of a petty bourgeois in revolt. In this sense one may say he has spoken the last word of bourgeois individualism."

Bakounine and Kropotkine, the famous Russian anarchists, are exposed as confused idealists, who have not aided but rather hindered the development of the working-class movement. Lenin speaks highly of the book in this relation, but takes Plechanoff severely to task for his failure properly to set forth the Marxian concepts of the State, and for his total evasion of the form the State must take during the time it is in the hands of the workers. When writing on the "Vulgarisation of Marx by the Opportunists," in his *State and Revolution*, Lenin said:

"Plechanoff devoted a special pamphlet to the question of the relation of socialism to anarchism entitled *Anarchism and Socialism*, published in German in 1894. He managed somehow to treat the question without touching on the most vital, controversial point, the essential point *politically*, in the struggle with the anarchists: the relation of the revolution to State, and the question of the State in general. His pamphlet may be divided into two parts: one, historico-literary, containing valuable material for the history of the ideas of Stirner, Proudhon, and others; the second, ignorant and narrow-minded, containing a clumsy disquisition on the theme 'that an anarchist [9] cannot be distinguished from a bandit,' an amusing combination of subjects and most characteristic of the entire activity of Plechanoff on the eve of revolution and during the revolutionary period in Russia. Indeed, in the years 1908 to 1917 Plechanoff showed himself to be half doctrinaire and half philistine, walking, politically, in the wake of the bourgeoisie.

"We saw how Marx and Engels, in their polemics against the anarchists, explained most thoroughly their views on the relation of the revolution to the State. Engels, when editing in 1891, Marx's *Criticism of the Gotha Program*, wrote that 'we'—that is, Engels and Marx—'were then in the fiercest phase of our battle with Bakounine and his anarchists; hardly two years had then passed since the Hague Congress of the International' (the First). The anarchists had tried to claim the Paris Commune as their 'own,' as a confirmation of their teachings, thus showing that they had not in the least understood the lessons of the Commune or the analysis of those lessons by Marx. Anarchism has given nothing approaching a true solution of the concrete political problems: are we to *break* up the old State machine, and what shall we put in its place?

"But to speak of *Anarchism and Socialism*, leaving the whole question of the State out of account and taking no notice at all of the whole development of Marxism before and after the Commune—that meant an inevitable fall into the pit of opportunism. For that is just what opportunism wants—to keep these two questions in [10] abeyance. To secure this is, in itself, a victory of opportunism."

The anarchist desire to abolish the State at one blow, and to abolish money, etc., in much the same way, springs from their inability to understand the institutions of capitalist society. To many of them the State is simply the result of people having faith in authority. Give up this belief and the State will cease to exist. It is a myth like God and rests entirely on faith. The anarchist's desire for the abolition of the State arises from entirely different concepts to that of the communists. To these anarchist anti-authoritarians the State is simply bad. It is the most authoritarian thing in sight. It interferes with individual freedom and consequently is the greatest obstruction to "absolute liberty" and other utopian desires of the champions of individualism.

Communists also want a society without a State but realize that such can only come about when society is without classes. The aim of the communist movement is to destroy the capitalist form of the State and substitute a proletarian form during the time in which society is undergoing its classless transformation. When all property is centralized into the hands of this working-class "State" and when the administration of things has taken the place of political dominance, the State, in its final form, will have withered away. Therefore, the communist realizes that the State cannot be abolished in the manner visualized by anarchists, but that it must be used, that is, the proletariat must be raised "to the [11] position of ruling class," for the purpose of expropriating the capitalists and putting an end to the exploitation of the producing class. The State is not abolished. Only its capitalist form is abolished. The State dies out in the hands of the workers when there is no longer an opposing class to coerce.
[12]
[13]

PREFACE.

The work of my friend George Plechanoff, "Anarchism and Socialism," was written originally in French. It was then translated into German by Mrs. Bernstein, and issued in pamphlet form by the German Social-Democratic Publishing Office "Vorwärts." It was next translated by myself into English, and so much of the translation as exigencies of space would permit, published in the *Weekly Times and Echo*. The original French version is now appearing in the *Jeunesse Socialiste*, and will be issued in book form shortly. The complete English translation is now given to English readers through the Twentieth Century Press. I have to thank the Editor of the *Weekly Times and Echo*, Mr. Kibblewhite, for his kindness in allowing me to use those portions of the work that appeared in his paper.

As to the book itself. There are those who think that the precious time of so remarkable a writer, and profound a thinker as George Plechanoff is simply wasted in pricking Anarchist windbags. But, unfortunately, there are many of the younger, or of the more ignorant sort, who are inclined to take words for deeds, high-sounding phrases for acts, mere sound and fury for revolutionary activity, and who are too [14] young or too ignorant to know that such sound and fury signify nothing. It is for the sake of these younger, or for the sake of the more ignorant, folk, that men like Plechanoff deal seriously with this matter of Anarchism, and do not feel their time lost if they can, as this work must, help readers to see the true meaning of what is called "Anarchism."

And a work like this one of Plechanoff's is doubly necessary in

England, where the Socialist movement is still largely disorganised, where there is still such ignorance and confusion on all economic and political subjects; where, with the exception, among the larger Socialist organisations, of the Social-Democratic Federation (and even among the younger S.D.F. members there is a vague sort of idea that Anarchism is something fine and revolutionary), there has been no little coquetting with Anarchism under an impression that it was very "advanced," and where the Old Unionist cry of "No politics!" has unconsciously played the reactionary Anarchist game. We cannot afford to overlook the fact that the Socialist League became in time—when some of us had left it—an Anarchist organisation, and that since then its leaders have been, or still are, more or less avowed Anarchists. While quite recently the leader of a "new party"—and that a would-be political one!—did not hesitate to declare his Anarchist sympathies or to state that "The methods of the Anarchists might differ from those of the Socialists, but that might only prove that the former were more zealous than the latter."

[15]

It is also necessary to point out once again that Anarchism and Nihilism have no more in common than Anarchism and Socialism. As Plechanoff said at the Zürich International Congress: "We (*i.e.*, the Russians) have had to endure every form of persecution, every thinkable misery; but we have been spared one disgrace, one humiliation; we, at least, have no Anarchists." A statement endorsed and emphasised by other Russian revolutionists, and notably by the American delegate, Abraham Cahan—himself a Russian refugee. The men and women who are waging their heroic war in Russia and in Poland against Czarism have no more in common with Anarchism than had the founders of the modern Socialist movement—Carl Marx and Frederick Engels.

This little book of Plechanoff will assuredly convince the youngest even that under any circumstances Anarchism is but another word for reaction; and the more honest the men and women who play this reactionist game, the more tragic and dangerous it becomes for the whole working class movement.

Finally, there is a last reason why the issuing of this work at the present moment is timely. In 1896 the next International Socialist and Trade Union Congress meets in London. It is well that those who may attend this great Congress as delegates, and that the thousands of workers who will watch its work, should understand why the resolutions arrived at by the Paris, Brussels, and Zürich International Congresses with regard to the Anarchists should [16] be enforced. The Anarchists who cynically declare Workers' Congresses "absurd, motiveless, and senseless" must be taught once and for all, that they cannot be allowed to make the Congresses of the Revolutionary Socialists of the whole world a playground for reaction and international spydom.

Eleanor Marx Aveling .

Green Street Green, Orpington, Kent. August, 1895.

[17]

ANARCHISM AND SOCIALISM

CHAPTER I

THE POINT OF VIEW OF THE UTOPIAN SOCIALISTS

The French Materialists of the 18th century while waging relentless war against all the "*infâmes*" whose yoke weighed upon the French of this period, by no means scorned the search after what they called "perfect legislation," *i.e.*, the best of all possible legislations, such legislation as should secure to "human beings" the greatest sum of happiness, and could be alike applicable to all existing societies, for the simple reason that it was "perfect" and therefore the most "natural." Excursions into this domain of "perfect legislation" occupy no small place in the works of a d'Holbach and a Helvétius. On the other hand, the Socialists of the first half of our century threw themselves with immense zeal, with unequalled perseverance, into the search after the best of possible social organisations, after a perfect social organisation. This is a striking and notable characteristic which they have in common with the French Materialists of the last century, and it is this characteristic which especially demands our attention in the present work.

[18]

In order to solve the problem of a perfect social organisation, or what comes to the same thing, of the best of all possible legislation, we must eventually have some criterion by the help of which we may compare the various "legislations" one with the other. And the criterion must have a special attribute. In fact, there is no question of a "legislation" *relatively* the best, *i.e.*, *the best legislation under given conditions*. No, indeed! We have to find a *perfect* legislation, a legislation whose perfection should have nothing relative about it, should be entirely independent of time and place, should be, in a word, absolute. We are therefore driven to make abstraction from history, since everything in history is relative, everything depends upon circumstance, time, and place. But abstraction made of the history of humanity, what is there left to guide us in our "legislative" investigations? Humanity is left us, man in general, human nature—of which history is but the manifestation. Here then we have our criterion definitely settled, a perfect legislation. The best of all possible legislation is that which best harmonises with human nature. It may be, of course, that even when we have such a criterion we may, for want of "light" or of logic, fail to solve this problem of the best legislation. *Errare humanum est*, but it seems incontrovertible that this problem *can* be solved, that we can, by taking our stand upon an exact knowledge of human nature, find a perfect legislation, a perfect organisation.

Such was, in the domain of social science, the [19] point of view of the French Materialists. Man is a sentient and reasonable being, they said; he avoids painful sensations and seeks pleasurable ones. He has sufficient intelligence to recognise what is useful to him as well as what is harmful to him. Once you admit these axioms, and you can in your investigations into the best legislation, arrive, with the help of reflection and good intentions, at conclusions as well founded, as exact, as incontrovertible as those derived from a mathematical demonstration. Thus Condorcet undertook to construct deductively all precepts of healthy morality by starting from the truth that man is a sentient and reasonable being.

It is hardly necessary to say that in this Condorcet was mistaken. If the "philosophers" in this branch of their investigations arrived at conclusions of incontestable though very relative value, they unconsciously owed this to the fact that they constantly abandoned their abstract standpoint of human nature in general, and took up that of a more or less idealised nature of a man of the Third Estate. This man "felt" and "reasoned," after a fashion very clearly defined by his social environment. It was his "nature" to believe firmly in bourgeois property, representative government, freedom of trade (*laissez-faire, laissez passer!* the "nature" of this man was always crying out), and so on. In reality, the French philosophers always kept in view the economic and political requirements of the Third Estate; this was their real criterion. But they applied it unconsciously, and only after much [20] wandering in the field of abstraction did they arrive at it. Their conscious method always reduced itself to abstract considerations of "human nature," and of the social and political institutions that best harmonise with this nature.

Their method was also that of the Socialists. A man of the 18th century, Morelly, "to anticipate a mass of empty objections that would be endless," lays down as an incontrovertible principle "that in morals nature is one, constant, invariable . that its laws never change;" and that "everything that may be advanced as to the variety in the morals of savage and civilised peoples, by no means proves that nature varies;" that at the outside it only shows "that from certain accidental causes which are foreign to it, some nations have fallen away from the laws of nature; others have remained submissive to them, in some respects from mere habit; finally, others are subjected to them by certain reasoned-out laws that are not always in contradiction with nature;" in a word, "man may abandon the True, but the True can never be annihilated!" [1] .... 6 Fourier relies upon the analysis of the human passions; Robert Owen starts from certain considerations on the formation of human character; Saint Simon, despite his deep comprehension of the historical evolution of humanity, constantly returns to "human nature" in order to explain the laws of this evolution; [21] the Saint-Simonians declared their philosophy was "based upon a new conception of human nature. " The Socialists of the various schools may quarrel as to the cause of their different conceptions of human nature; all, without a single exception, are convinced that social science has not and cannot have, any other basis than an adequate concept of this nature. In this they in no wise differ from the Materialists of the 18th century. Human nature is the one criterion they invariably apply in their criticism of existing society, and in their search after a social organisation as it should be, after a "perfect" legislation.

Morelly, Fourier, Saint Simon, Owen— we look upon all of them to-day as Utopian Socialists. Since we know the general point of view that is common to them all, we can determine exactly what the Utopian point of view is. This will be the more useful, seeing that the opponents of Socialism use the word "Utopian" without attaching to it any, even approximately, definite meaning.

The *Utopian is one who, starting from an abstract principle, seeks for a perfect social organisation*.

The abstract principle which served as starting point of the Utopians was that of human nature. Of course there have been Utopians who applied the principle indirectly through the intermediary of concepts derived from it. Thus, *e.g.*, in seeking for "perfect legislation," for an ideal organisation of society, one may start from the concept of the Rights of Man. But it is [22] evident that in its ultimate analysis this concept derives from that of human nature.

It is equally evident that one may be a Utopian without being a Socialist. The bourgeois tendencies of the French Materialists of the last century are most noticeable in their investigations of a perfect legislation. But this in no wise destroys the Utopian character of these enquires. We have seen that the method of the Utopian Socialist does not in the least differ from that of d'Holbach or Helvétius, those champions of the revolutionary French bourgeoisie.

Nay, more. One may have the profoundest contempt for all "music of the future," one may be convinced that the social world in which one has the good fortune to live is the best possible of all social worlds, and yet in spite of this one may look at the structure and life of the body social from the same point of view as that from which the Utopians regarded it.

This seems a paradox, and yet nothing could be more true. Take but one example.

In 1753 there appeared Morelly's work, *Les Isles Flottantes ou la Basiliade du célébre Pelpai, traduit de l'Indien*. [2] Now, note the arguments with which a review, *La Bibliothèque Impartiale*, combated the communistic ideas of the author:—"One knows well enough that a distance separates the finest speculations of this kind and the possibility of their realisation. For in theory [23] one takes imaginary men who lend themselves obediently to every arrangement, and who second with equal zeal the views of the legislator; but as soon as one attempts to put these things into practice one has to deal with men as they are, that is to say, submissive, lazy, or else in the thraldom of some violent passion. The scheme of equality especially is one that seems most repugnant to the nature of man; they are born to command or to serve, a middle term is a burden to them."

Men are born to command or to serve. We cannot wonder, therefore, if in society we see masters and servants, since human nature wills it so. It was all very well for *La Bibliothèque Impartiale* to repudiate these communist speculations. The point of view from which it itself looked upon social phenomena, the point of view of human nature, it had in common with the Utopian Morelly.

And it cannot be urged that this review was probably not sincere in its arguments, and that it appealed to human nature with the single object of saying something in favour of the exploiters, in favour of those who "command." But sincere or hypocritical in its criticism of Morelly, the *Bibliothèque Impartiale* adopted the standpoint common to all the writers of this period. They all of them appeal to human nature conceived of in one form or another, with the sole exception of the retrogrades who, living shadows of passed times, continued to appeal to the will of God.

As we know, this concept of human nature has [24] been inherited by the 19th century from its predecessor. The Utopian Socialists had no other. But here again it is easy to prove that it is not peculiar to the Utopians.

Even at the period of the Restoration, the eminent French historian, Guizot, in his historical studies, arrived at the remarkable conclusion that the political constitution of any given country depended upon the "condition of property" in that country. This was an immense advance upon the ideas of the last century which had almost exclusively considered the action of the "legislator." But what in its turn did these "conditions of property" depend on? Guizot is unable to answer this question, and after long, vain efforts to find a solution of the enigma in historical circumstances, he returns, falls back *nolens volens*, upon the theory of human nature. Augustin Thierry, another eminent historian of the Restoration, found himself in almost the same case, or rather he would have done so if only he had tried to investigate this question of the "condition of property" and its historical vicissitudes. In his concept of social life, Thierry was never able to go beyond his master Saint Simon, who, as we have seen above, held firmly to the point of view of human nature.

The example of the brilliant Saint Simon, a man of encyclopædic learning, demonstrates more clearly perhaps than any other, how narrow and insufficient was this point of view, in what confusion worse confounded of contradictions it landed those who applied it. Says Saint Simon, with the profoundest conviction: "The future is [25] made up of the last terms of a series, the first of which consist of the past. When one has thoroughly mastered the first terms of any series it is easy to put down their successors; thus from the past carefully observed one can easily deduce the future." This is so true that one asks oneself at the first blush why a man who had so clear a conception of the connection between the various phases of historical evolution, should be classed among the Utopians. And yet, look more closely at the historical ideas of Saint Simon, and you will find that we are not wrong in calling him a Utopian. The future is deducible from the past, the historical evolution of humanity is a process governed by law. But what is the impetus, the motive power that sets in motion the human species, that makes it pass from one phase of its evolution to another? Of what does this impetus consist? Where are we to seek it? It is here that Saint Simon comes back to the point of view of all the Utopians, to the point of view of human nature. Thus, according to him, the essential fundamental cause of the French Revolution was a change in the temporal and spiritual forces, and, in order to direct it wisely and conclude it rightly, it "was necessary to put into direct political activity the forces which had become preponderant." In other words, the manufacturers and the *savants* ought to have been called upon to formulate a political system corresponding to the new social conditions. This was not done, and the Revolution which had began so well was almost immediately directed into a false path. [26] The lawyers and metaphysicians became the masters of the situation. How to explain this historical fact? "It is in the nature of man," replies Saint Simon, "to be unable to pass without some intermediate phase from any one doctrine to another. This law applies most stringently to the various political systems, through which the natural advance of civilisation compels the human species to pass. Thus the same necessity which in industry has created the element of a new temporal power, destined to replace military power, and which in the positive sciences, has created the element of a new spiritual power, called upon to take the place of theological power, must have developed and set in activity (before the change in the conditions of society had begun to be very perceptible) a temporal or spiritual power of an intermediary, bastard, and transitory nature, whose only mission was to bring about the transition from one social system to another."

So we see that the "historical series" of Saint Simon really explained nothing at all; they themselves need explanation, and for this we have again to fall back upon this inevitable human nature. The French Revolution was directed along a certain line, because human nature was so and so.

One of two things. Either human nature is, as Morelly thought, invariable, and then it explains nothing in history, which shows us constant variations in the relations of man to society; or it does vary according to the circumstances in which men live, and then, far from [27] being the *cause*, it is itself the *effect* of historical evolution. The French Materialists knew well enough that man is the product of his social surroundings. "Man is all education," said Helvétius. This would lead one to suppose that Helvétius must have abandoned the human nature point of view in order to study the laws of the evolution of the environment that fashion human nature, giving to socialised man such or such an "education." And indeed Helvétius did make some efforts in this direction. But not he, nor his contemporaries, nor the Socialists of the first half of our century, nor any representatives of science of the same period, succeeded in discovering a new point of view that should permit the study of the evolution of the social environment; the cause of the historical "education" of man, the cause of the changes which occur in his "nature." They were thus forced back upon the human nature point of view as the only one that seemed to supply them with a fairly solid basis for their scientific investigations. But since human nature in its turn varied, it became indispensable to make abstraction from its variations, and to seek in nature only stable properties, fundamental properties preserved in spite of all changes of its secondary properties. And in the end all that these speculations resulted in was a meagre abstraction, like that of the philosophers, *e.g.*, "man is a sentient and reasonable being," which seemed all the more precious a discovery in that it left plenty of room for every gratuitous hypothesis, and every fantastical conclusion.

[28]

A Guizot had no need to seek for the best of social organisations for a perfect legislation. He was perfectly satisfied with the existing ones. And assuredly the most powerful argument he could have advanced to defend them from the attacks of the malcontents would still have been human nature, which he would have said renders every serious change in the social and political constitution of France impossible. The malcontents condemned this same constitution, making use of the same abstraction. And since this abstraction, being completely empty, left, as we have said, full room for every gratuitous hypothesis and the logical consequences resulting therefrom, the "scientific" mission of these reformers assumed the appearance of a geometrical problem; given a certain nature, find what structure of society best corresponds with it. So Morelly complains bitterly because "our old teachers" failed to attempt the solution of "this excellent problem"—"to find the condition in which it should be almost impossible for men to be depraved, or wicked, or at any rate, *minima de malis*." We have already seen that for Morelly human nature was "one, constant, invariable."

We now know what was the "scientific" method of the Utopians. Before we leave them let us remind the reader that in human nature, an extremely thin and therefore not very satisfying abstraction, the Utopians really appealed, not to human nature in general, but to the idealised nature of the men of their own day, belonging to the class whose social tendencies they [29] represented. The social reality, therefore, inevitably appears in the words of the Utopians, but the Utopians were unconscious of this. They saw this reality only across an abstraction which, thin as it was, was by no means translucent.

FOOTNOTES:

[1] See "Code de la Nature," Paris, 1841. Villegardelle's edition, Note to p. 66.

[2] "The floating islands or the Basiliades of the celebrated Pelpai, translated from the Indian."

[30]

CHAPTER II

THE POINT OF VIEW OF SCIENTIFIC SOCIALISM

The great idealistic philosophers of Germany, Schelling and Hegel, understood the insufficiency of the human nature point of view. Hegel, in his "Philosophy of History," makes fun of the Utopian bourgeoisie in search of the best of constitutions. German Idealism conceived history as a process subject to law, and sought the motive-power of the historical movement *outside the nature of man*. This was a great step towards the truth. But the Idealists saw this motive-power in the absolute idea, in the "Weltgeist;" and as their absolute idea was only an abstraction of "our process of thinking," in their philosophical speculation upon history, they reintroduced the old love of the Materialist philosophers—human nature—but dressed in robes worthy of the respectable and austere society of German thinkers. Drive nature out of the door, she flies in at the window! Despite the great services rendered to social science by the German Idealists, the great problem of that science, its essential problem, was no more solved in the time of the German Idealists than in the time of the French Materialists. What is this hidden force that causes the historic movement [31] of humanity? No one knew anything about it. In this field there was nothing to go upon save a few isolated observations, more or less accurate, more or less ingenious—sometimes indeed, very accurate and ingenious—but always disjointed and always incomplete.

That social science at last emerged from this No Thoroughfare, it owes to Karl Marx.

According to Marx, "legal relations, like forms of State, can neither be understood in themselves nor from the so-called general development of the human mind, but are rather rooted in those material conditions of life, whose totality Hegel, following the English and the French of the 18th century, summed up under the name of 'bourgeois society.'" This is almost the same as Guizot meant when he said that political constitutions had their roots in "the condition of property." But while for Guizot "the condition of property" remained a mystery which he vainly sought to elucidate with the help of reflections upon human nature, for Marx this "condition" had nothing mysterious; it is determined by the condition of the productive forces at the disposal of a given society. "The anatomy of bourgeois society is to be sought in political economy." But Marx himself shall formulate his own conception of history.

"In the social production of their lives, men enter upon certain definite, necessary relations, relations independent of their will, relations of production that correspond with definite degrees of development of their material productive forces. The totality of these relations of] [32] production constitute the economic structure of society, the true basis from which arises a juridical and political superstructure to which definite social forms of consciousness correspond. The mode of production of material life determines the social, political and intellectual processes of life.

It is not the consciousness of mankind that determines their being, but, on the contrary, their social being that determines their consciousness. In a certain stage of their development, the material forces of production of society come into contradiction with the existing relations of production, or, which is only a juridical expression for the same thing, with the relations of property within which they had hitherto moved. From forms for the development of these forces of production, they are transformed into their fetters. We then enter upon an epoch of social revolution." [3]

This completely materialist conception of history is one of the greatest discoveries of our century, so rich in scientific discoveries. Thanks to it alone sociology has at last, and for ever, escaped from the vicious circle in which it had, until then, turned; thanks to it alone this science now possesses a foundation as solid as natural science. The revolution made by Marx in social science may be compared with that made by Kopernicus in astronomy. In fact, before Kopernicus, it was believed that the earth remained stationary, while the sun turned round it. The [33] Polish genius demonstrated that what occurred was the exact contrary. And so, up to the time of Marx, the point of view taken by social science, was that of "human nature;" and it was from this point of view that men attempted to explain the historical movement of humanity. To this the point of view of the German genius is diametrically opposed. While man, in order to maintain his existence, acts upon nature outside himself, he alters his own nature. The action of man upon the nature outside himself, pre-supposes certain instruments, certain means of production; according to the character of their means of production men enter into certain relations within the process of production (since this process is a social one), and according to their relations in this social process of production, their habits, their sentiments, their desires, their methods of thought and of action, in a word, their nature, vary. Thus it is not human nature which explains the historical movement; it is the historical movement which fashions diversely human nature.

But if this is so, what is the value of all the more or less laborious, more or less ingenious enquiries into "perfect legislation" and the best of possible social organisations? None; literally none! They can but bear witness to the lack of scientific education in those who pursue them. Their day is gone for ever. With this old point of view of human nature must disappear the Utopias of every shade and colour. The great revolutionary party of our day, the International Social-Democracy, is based not upon some "new [34] conception" of human nature, nor upon any abstract principle, but upon a scientifically demonstrable economic necessity. And herein lies the real strength of this party, making it as invincible as the economic necessity itself.

"The means of production and exchange on whose foundation the bourgeoisie built itself up, were generated in feudal society. At a certain stage in the development of these means of production and exchange, the conditions under which feudal society produced and exchanged, the feudal organisation of agriculture and manufacturing industry, in one word, the feudal relations of property become no longer compatible with the already developed productive forces, they become so many fetters. They had to be burst asunder; they were burst asunder. Into their place stepped free competition, accompanied by a social and political constitution adapted to it, and by the economical and political sway of the bourgeois class. A similar movement is going on before our own eyes. Modern bourgeois society, with its relations of production, of exchange, and of property, a society that has conjured up such gigantic means of production and of exchange, is like the sorcerer, who is no longer able to control the powers of the nether world whom he has called up by his spells. For many a decade past the history of industry and commerce is but the history of the revolt of modern productive forces against the property relations that are the conditions for the existence of the bourgeoisie and its rule. It is enough to mention the commercial crises that by their [35] periodical return put on its trial, each time more threateningly, the existence of the entire bourgeois society. The weapons with which the bourgeoisie felled feudalism to the ground are now turned against the bourgeoisie itself." [4]

The bourgeoisie destroyed the feudal conditions of property; the proletariat will put an end to the bourgeois conditions of property. Between the proletariat and the bourgeoisie a struggle, an implacable war, a war to the knife, is as inevitable as, was in its way, the struggle between the bourgeoisie and the privileged estates. *But every class war is a political war.* In order to do away with feudal society the bourgeoisie had to seize upon political power. In order to do away with capitalist society the proletariat must do the same. Its political task is therefore traced out for it beforehand by the force of events themselves, and not by any abstract consideration.

It is a remarkable fact that it is only since Karl Marx that Socialism has taken its stand upon the class war. The Utopian Socialists had no notion—even an inexact one—of it. And in this they lagged behind their contemporary theorists of the bourgeoisie, who understood very well the historical significance at any rate of the struggle of the third estate against the nobles.

If every "new conception" of human nature [36] seemed to supply very definite indications as to the organisation of "the society of the future," Scientific Socialism is very chary of such speculations. The structure of society depends upon the conditions of its productive forces. What these conditions will be when the proletariat is in power we do not know. We now know but one thing—that the productive forces already at the disposal of civilised humanity imperatively demand the socialisation and systematised organisation of the means of production. This is enough to prevent our being led astray in our struggle against "the reactionary mass." "The Communists, therefore, are practically the most advanced and resolute section of the working class parties of every country. theoretically they have over the great mass of the proletariat the advantage of clearly understanding the line of march, the conditions, and the ultimate general results of the proletarian movement." [5] These words, written in 1848, are to-day incorrect only in one sense: they speak of "working class parties" independent of the Communist party; there is to-day no working class party which does not more or less closely follow the flag of Scientific Socialism, or, as it was called in the Manifesto, "Communism."

Once again, then, the point of view of the Utopian Socialists, as indeed of all social science of their time, was human nature, or some abstract principle deriving from this idea. The point of view of the social science, of the Socialism of [37] our time is that of economic reality, and of the immanent laws of its evolution.

It is easy, therefore, to form an idea of the impression made upon modern Socialists by the arguments of the bourgeois theorists who sing ceaselessly the same old song of the incompatibility of human nature and communism. It is as though one would wage war upon the Darwinians with arms drawn from the scientific arsenal of Cuvier's time. And a most noteworthy fact is that the "evolutionists" like Herbert Spencer, themselves are not above piping to the same tune. [6]

And now let us see what relation there may be between modern Socialism and what is called Anarchism.

FOOTNOTES:

[3] "Zur Kritik der Politischen Œkonomie," Berlin, 1859. Preface iv. v.

[4] "Manifesto of the Communist Party." By Karl Marx and Frederick Engels. Authorised English translation by S. Moore, pp. 11-12.

[5] "Communist Manifesto," p. 16.

[6] "The belief not only of the Socialists, but also of those so-called Liberals who are diligently preparing the way for them, is that by due skill an ill-working humanity may be framed into well-working institutions. It is a delusion. The defective nature of citizens will show themselves in the bad acting of whatever social structure they are arranged into. There is no political alchemy by which you can get golden conduct out of leaden instincts."—Herbert Spencer's "The Man *versus* the State," p. 43.

[38]

CHAPTER III

THE HISTORICAL DEVELOPMENT OF THE ANARCHIST DOCTRINE

The Point of View of Anarchism.

"I have often been reproached with being the father of Anarchism. This is doing me too great an honour. The father of Anarchism is the immortal Proudhon, who expounded it for the first time in 1848."

Thus spoke Peter Kropotkin in his defence before the Correctional Tribunal of Lyons at his trial in January, 1883. As is frequently the case with my amiable compatriot, Kropotkin has here made a statement that is incorrect. For "the first time" Proudhon spoke of Anarchism was in his celebrated book "*Qu'est-ce que le Propriété, ou Recherches sur le principe du droit et du Gouvernement*," the first edition of which had already appeared in 1840. It is true that he "expounds" very little of it here; he only devotes a few pages to it. [7] And before he set about expounding the Anarchist theory "in 1848," the job had already been done by a German, Max Stirner (the pseudonym of Caspar Schmidt) in 1845, in his book "Der Einzige und [39] sein Eigenthum." [8] Max Stirner has therefore a well defined claim to be the father of Anarchism. "Immortal" or not, it is by him that the theory was "expounded" *for the first time*.

Max Stirner

The Anarchist theory of Max Stirner has been called a caricature of the "philosophy of religion" of Ludwig Feuerbach. It is thus, *e.g.*, that Ueberweg in his "Grundzüge der Geschichte der Philosophie," (3rd. part, "Philosophie der Neu Zeit") speaks of it. Some have even supposed that the only object Stirner had in writing his book was to poke fun at this philosophy. This supposition is absolutely gratuitous. Stirner in expounding his theory was not joking. He is in deadly earnest about it, though he now and again betrays a tendency, natural enough in the restless times when he wrote, to outdo Feuerbach and the radical character of his conclusions.

For Feuerbach, what men call Divinity, is only the product of their phantasy, of a psychological aberration. It is not Divinity that has created man, but man who creates Divinity in his own image. In God man only adores his own being. God is only a fiction, but a very harmful fiction. The Christian God is supposed to be all love, all pity for poor suffering humanity. But in spite of this, or rather *because of it*, every Christian really worthy the name, hates, and must hate, the Atheists, who appear to him the living [40] negation of all love and all pity. Thus the god of love becomes the god of hate, the god of persecution; the product of the phantasy of man becomes a real cause of his suffering. So we must make an end of this phantasmagoria. Since in Divinity man adores only his own being, we must once for all rend and scatter to the winds the mystic veil beneath which this being has been enveloped. The love of humanity must not extend beyond humanity. "Der Mensch ist dem Menschen das höchste Wesen" (Man is the highest being for man).

Thus Feuerbach. Max Stirner is quite at one with him, but wishes to deduce what he believes to be the final, the most radical consequences of his theory. He reasons in this fashion. God is only the product of phantasy, is only a *spook*. Agreed. But what is this humanity the love of which you prescribe to me? Is not this also a spook, an abstract thing, a creature of the imagination? Where is this humanity of yours? Where does it exist but in the minds of men, in the minds of individuals? The only reality, therefore, is the *individual*, with his wants, his tendencies, his will. But since this is so, how can the *individual*, the reality, sacrifice himself for the happiness of man, an abstract being? It is all very well for you to revolt against the old God; you still retain the religious point of view, and the emancipation you are trying to help us to is absolutely theological, *i.e.*, "God-inspired." "The highest Being is certainly that of man, but because it is his *Being* and is not he himself, it is quite [41] indifferent if we see this Being outside of him as God, or find it in him and call it the 'Being of Mankind' or 'Man.' *I* am neither God nor Man, neither the highest Being, nor my own Being, and therefore it is essentially a matter of indifference if I imagine this Being in myself or outside myself. And, indeed, we do always imagine the highest being in the two future states, in the internal and external at once; for the 'Spirit of God' is, according to the Christian conception, also 'our spirit' and 'dwells within us.' It dwells in heaven and dwells in us; but we poor things are but its 'dwelling-place,' and if Feuerbach destroys its heavenly dwelling-place and forces it to come down to us bag and baggage, we, its earthly abode, will find ourselves very over-crowded." [9]

To escape the inconveniences of such over-crowding, to avoid being dominated by any spook, to at last place our foot upon actual ground, there is but one way: to take as our starting-point the only real being, our own Ego, "Away then with everything that is not wholly and solely my own affair! You think my own concerns must at least be 'good ones?' A fig for good and evil! I am I, and I am neither good nor evil. Neither has any meaning for me. The godly is the affair of God, the human that of humanity. My concern is neither the Godly nor the Human, is not the True, the Good, the [42] Right, the Free, etc., but simply my own self, and it is not general, it is individual, as I myself am individual. For me there is nothing above myself." [10]

Religion, conscience, morality, right, law, family, state, are but so many fetters forced upon me in the name of an abstraction, but so many despotic lords whom "I," the individual conscious of my own "concerns," combat by every means in my power. Your "*morality*," not merely the morality of the bourgeois philistines, but the most elevated, the most humanitarian morality is only religion which has changed its supreme beings. Your "*right*," that you believe born with man, is but a ghost, and if you respect it, you are no farther advanced than the heroes of Homer who were afraid when they beheld a god fighting in the ranks of their enemies. Right is might. "Whoever has might, he has right; if you have not the former you have not the latter. Is this wisdom so difficult of attainment?" [11] You would persuade me to sacrifice my interests to those of the State. I, on the contrary, declare war to the knife to all States, even the most democratic. "Every State is a despotism, whether it is the despotism of one or many, or whether, as one might suppose would be the case in a Republic, all are masters, *i.e.*, one tyrannises over the rest. For this is the case whenever a given law, the expressed will perhaps of some assemblage of the [43] people, is immediately to become a law to the individual, which he must obey, and which it is his *duty* to obey. Even if one were to suppose a case in which every individual among the people had expressed the same will, and thus a perfect "will of all" had easily been arrived at, the thing would still be the same. Should I not to-day and in the future be bound by my will of yesterday? In this event my will would be paralyzed. Fatal stagnation! My creation, *i.e.*, a certain expression of will would have become my master. But I, in my will should be constrained, I, the creator should be constrained in my development, my working out. Because I was a fool yesterday, I must remain one all my life. So that in my life in relation to the State I am at best—I might as well say at worst—a slave to my own self. Because yesterday I had a will, I am to-day without one; yesterday free, to-day bound." [12]

Here a partisan of the "People's State" might observe to Stirner, that his "I" goes a little too far in his desire to reduce democratic liberty to absurdity; further, that a bad law may be abrogated as soon as a majority of citizens desire it, and that one is not forced to submit to it "all one's life." But this is only an insignificant detail, to which, moreover, Stirner would reply that the very necessity for appealing to a majority proves that "I" am no longer the master of my own conduct. The conclusions of our author are irrefutable, for the simple reason that [44] to say, I recognize nothing above myself, is to say, I feel oppressed by every institution that imposes any duty upon me. It is simply tautology.

It is evident that no "Ego" can exist quite alone. Stirner knows this perfectly, and this is why he advocates "Leagues of Egoists," that is to say, free associations into which every "Ego" enters, and in which he remains when and so long as it suits his interests.

Here let us pause. We are now face to face with an "egoist" system *par excellence*. It is, perhaps, the only one that the history of human thought has to chronicle. The French Materialists of the last century have been accused of preaching egoism. The accusation was quite wrong. The French Materialists always preached "Virtue," and preached it with such unlimited zeal that Grimm could, not without reason, make fun of their *capucinades* on the subject. The question of egoism presented to them a double problem. (1) Man is all sensation (this was the basis of all their speculations upon man); by his very nature he is forced to shun suffering and to seek pleasure; how comes it then that we find men capable of enduring the greatest sufferings for the sake of some idea, that is to say, in its final analysis, in order to provide agreeable sensations for their fellow-men. (2) Since man is all sensation he will harm his fellow-man if he is placed in a social environment where the interests of an individual conflict with those of others. What form of legislation therefore can harmonise public good [45] and that of individuals? Here, in this double problem, lies the whole significance of what is called the materialist ethics of the 18th century. Max Stirner pursues an end entirely opposed to this. He laughs at "Virtue," and, far from desiring its triumph, he sees reasonable men only in egoists, for whom there is nothing above their own "Ego." Once again, he is the theorist *par excellence* of egoism.

The good bourgeois whose ears are as chaste and virtuous as their hearts are hard; they who, "drinking wine, publicly preach water," were scandalised to the last degree by the "immorality" of Stirner. "It is the complete ruin of the moral world," they cried. But as usual the virtue of the philistines showed itself very weak in argument. "The real merit of Stirner is that he has spoken the last word of the young atheist school" (*i. e.*, the left wing of the Hegelian school), wrote the Frenchman, St. Réné Taillandier. The philistines of other lands shared this view of the "merits" of the daring publicist. From the point of view of modern Socialism this "merit" appears in a very different light.

To begin with, the incontestable merit of Stirner consists in his having openly and energetically combated the sickly sentimentalism of the bourgeois reformers and of many of the Utopian Socialists, according to which the emancipation of the proletariat would be brought about by the virtuous activity of "devoted" persons of all classes, and especially of those of the possessing-class. Stirner knew perfectly what [46] to expect from the "devotion" of the exploiters. The "rich" are harsh, hard-hearted, but the "poor" (the terminology is that of our author) are wrong to complain of it, since it is not the rich who create the poverty of the poor, but the poor who create the wealth of the rich. They ought to blame themselves then if their condition is a hard one. In order to change it they have only to revolt against the rich; as soon as they seriously wish it, they will be the strongest and the reign of wealth will be at an end. Salvation lies in struggle, and not in fruitless appeals to the generosity of the oppressors. Stirner, therefore, preaches the class war. It is true that he represents it in the abstract form of the struggle of a certain number of egoist "Egos" against another smaller number of "Egos" not less egoist. But here we come to another merit of Stirner's.

According to Taillandier, he has spoken the last word of the young atheist school of German philosophers. As a matter of fact he has only spoken the last word of idealist speculation. But that word he has incontestably the merit of having spoken.

In his criticism of religion Feuerbach is but half a Materialist. In worshipping God, man only worships his own Being idealised. This is true. But religions spring up and die out, like everything else upon earth. Does this not prove that the human Being is not immutable, but changes in the process of the historical evolution of societies? Clearly, yes. But, then, what is the cause of the historical transformation of the [47] "human Being?" Feuerbach does not know. For him the human Being is only an abstract notion, as human Nature was for the French Materialists. This is the fundamental fault of his criticism of religion. Stirner said that it had no very robust constitution. He wished to strengthen it by making it breathe the fresh air of reality. He turns his back upon all phantoms, upon all things of the imagination. In reality, he said to himself, these are only individuals. Let us take the individual for our starting-point. But *what* individual does he take for his starting-point? Tom, Dick, or Harry? Neither. He takes the *individual in general*—he takes a new abstraction, the thinnest of them all—he takes the "Ego."

Stirner naïvely imagined that he was finally solving an old philosophical question, which had already divided the Nominalists and the Realists of the Middle Ages. "No Idea has an existence," he says, "for none is capable of becoming corporeal. The scholastic controversy of Realism and Nominalism had the same content." Alas! The first Nominalist he came across could have demonstrated to our author by the completest evidence, that his "Ego" is as much an "Idea" as any other, and that it is as little real as a mathematical unit.

Tom, Dick and Harry have relations with one another that do not depend upon the will of their "Ego," but are imposed upon them by the structure of the society in which they live. To criticise social institutions in the name of the "Ego," is therefore to abandon the only [48] profitable point of view in the case, *i.e.*, that of society, of the laws of its existence and evolution, and to lose oneself in the mists of abstraction. But it is just in these mists that the "Nominalist" Stirner delights. I am I—that is his starting-point; not I is not I—that is his result. I+I+I+etc.—is his social Utopia. It is subjective Idealism, pure and simple applied to social and political criticism. It is the suicide of idealist speculation.

But in the same year (1845) in which "Der Einzige" of Stirner appeared, there appeared also, at Frankfort-on-Maine the work of Marx and Engels, "Die heilige Familie, oder Kritik der Kritischen Kritik, gegen Bruno Bauer und Consorten." [13] In it Idealist speculation was attacked and beaten by Materialist dialectic, the theoretical basis of modern Socialism. "Der Einzige" came too late.

We have just said that I+I+I+etc. represents the social Utopia of Stirner. His League of Egoists is, in fact, nothing but a mass of abstract quantities. What are, what can be the basis of their union? Their interests, answers Stirner. But what will, what can be the true basis of any given combination of their interests? Stirner says nothing about it, and he can say nothing definite since from the abstract heights on which he stands, one cannot see clearly economic reality, the mother and nurse of all the "Egos," egoistic or altruistic. Nor is it [49] surprising that he is not able to explain clearly even this idea of the class struggle, of which he nevertheless had a happy inkling. The "poor" must combat the "rich." And after, when they have conquered these? Then every one of the former "poor," like every one of the former "rich," will combat every one of the former poor, and against every one of the former rich. There will be the war of all against all. (These are Stirner's own words.) And the rules of the "Leagues of Egoists" will be so many partial truces in this colossal and universal warfare. There is plenty of fight in this idea, but of the "realism" Max

Stirner dreamed of, nothing.

But enough of the "Leagues of Egoists." A Utopian may shut his eyes to economic reality, but it forces itself upon him in spite of himself; it pursues him everywhere with the brutality of a natural force not controlled by force. The elevated regions of the abstract "I" do not save Stirner from the attacks of economic reality. He does not speak to us only of the "Individual"; his theme is "the Individual *and his property*." Now, what sort of a figure does the property of the "Individual" cut?

It goes without saying, that Stirner is little inclined to respect property as an "acquired right." "Only that property will be legally and lawfully another's which it suits *you* should be his property. When it ceases to suit you, it has lost its legality for you, and any absolute right in it you will laugh at." [14] It is always the same tune: "For me there is nothing above myself." But his scant respect for the property of others does not prevent the "Ego" of Stirner from having the tendencies of a property-owner. The strongest argument against Communism, is, in his opinion, the consideration that Communism by abolishing individual property transforms all members of society into mere beggars. Stirner is indignant at such an iniquity.

"Communists think that the Commune should be the property-owner. On the contrary, *I* am a property-owner, and can only agree with others as to my property. If the Commune does not do as I wish I rebel against it, and defend my property, I am the owner of property, but property *is not sacred*. Should I only be the holder of property (an allusion to Proudhon)? No, hitherto one was only a holder of property, assured of possession of a piece of land, because one left others also in possession of a piece of land; but now *everything* belongs to me, I am the owner of *everything I need*, and can get hold of. If the Socialist says, society gives me what I need, the Egoist says, I take what I want. If the Communists behave like beggars, the Egoist behaves like an owner of property." [15] The property of the egoist seems pretty shaky. An "Egoist," retains his property only as long as the other "Egoists" do not care to take it from him, thus transforming him into a "beggar." But the devil is not so black as he is painted. Stirner pictures the mutual relations of the "Egoist" proprietors rather as relations of exchange than of pillage. And force, to which he constantly appeals, is rather the economic force of a producer of commodities freed from the trammels which the State and "Society" in general impose, or seem to impose, upon him.

It is the soul of a producer of commodities that speaks through the mouth of Stirner. If he falls foul of the State, it is because the State does not seem to respect the "property" of the producers of commodities sufficiently. He wants *his* property, his *whole* property. The State makes him pay taxes; it ventures to expropriate him for the public good. He wants a *jus utendi et abutendi*; the State says "agreed"—but adds that there are abuses and abuses. Then Stirner cries "stop thief!" "I am the enemy of the State," says he, "which is always fluctuating between the alternative: He or I. With the State there is no property, *i.e.*, no individual property, only State property. Only through the State have I what I have, as it is only through the State that I am what I am. My private property is only what the State leaves me of its own, while it deprives other citizens of it: that is State property." So down with the State and long live full and complete individual property!

Stirner translated into German J. B. Say's "Traité D'Economie Politique Pratique" (Leipsic, 1845-46). And although he also translated Adam Smith, he was never able to get beyond the narrow circle of the ordinary bourgeois economic ideas. His "League of Egoists" is only the Utopia of a petty bourgeois in revolt. In this sense one may say he has spoken the last word of bourgeois individualism.

Stirner has also a third merit—that of the courage of his opinions, of having carried through to the very end his individualist theories. He is the most intrepid, the most consequent of the Anarchists. By his side Proudhon, whom Kropotkin, like all the present day Anarchists, takes for the father of Anarchism, is but a straight-laced Philistine.

FOOTNOTES:

[7] See pages 295-305 of the 1841 edition.
[8] "The Individual and his Property."
[9] "Der Einzige und sein Eigenthum." 2nd ed., Leipzig, 1882, pp. 35-36. (American translation: "The Ego and his Own." New York: 1907.)
[10] Ibid. Pp. 7-8.
[11] Ibid. pp. 196-197.
[12] Ibid. p. 200.
[13] "The Holy Family, or Criticism of Critical Criticism, against Bruno Bauer and Company."
[14] Der Einzige und sein Eigenthum.
[15] Ibid. p. 266.

CHAPTER IV

PROUDHON

If Stirner combats Feuerbach, the "immortal" Proudhon imitates Kant. "What Kant did some sixty years ago for religion, what he did earlier for certainty of certainties; what others before him had attempted to do for happiness or supreme good, the 'Voice of the People' proposes to do for the Government," pompously declares "the father of Anarchism." Let us examine his methods and their results.

According to Proudhon, before Kant, the believer and the philosopher moved "by an irresistible impulse," asked themselves, "What is God?" They then asked themselves "Which, of all religions, is the best?" "In fact, if there does exist a Being superior to Humanity, there must also exist a system of the relations between this Being and Humanity. What then is this system? The search for the best religion is the second step that the human mind takes in reason and in faith. Kant gave up these insoluble questions. He no longer asked himself what is God, and which is the best religion, he set about explaining the origin and development of the Idea of God; he undertook to work out the biography of this idea." And the results he attained were [54] as great as they were unexpected. "What we seek, what we see, in God, as Malebranche said . is our own Ideal, the pure essence of Humanity. The human soul does not become conscious of its Ego through premeditated contemplation, as the psychologists put it; the soul perceives something outside itself, as if it were a different Being face to face with itself, and it is this inverted image which it calls God. Thus morality, justice, order, law, are no longer things revealed from above, imposed upon our free will by a so-called Creator, unknown and unununderstandable; they are things that are proper and essential to us as our faculties and our organs, as our flesh and our blood. In two words religion and society are synonymous terms, man is as sacred to himself as if he were God."

Belief in authority is as primitive, as universal as belief in God. Whenever men are grouped together in societies there is authority, the beginning of a government. From time immemorial men have asked themselves, What is authority? Which is the best form of government? And replies to these questions have been sought for in vain. There are as many governments as there are religions, as many political theories as systems of philosophy. Is there any way of putting an end to this interminable and barren controversy? Any means of escape from this *impasse*! Assuredly! We have only to follow the example of Kant. We have only to ask ourselves whence comes this idea of authority, of government? We have only to get all the [55] information we can upon the legitimacy of the political idea. Once safe on this ground and the question solves itself with extraordinary ease.

"Like religion, government is a manifestation of social spontaneity, a preparation of humanity for a higher condition."

"What humanity seeks in religion and calls God, is itself." "What the citizen seeks in Government and calls king, emperor, or president, is again himself, is liberty." "Outside humanity there is no God; the theological concept has no meaning:—outside liberty no government, the political concept has no value. "

So much for the "biography" of the political idea. Once grasped it must enlighten us upon the question as to which is the best form of government.

"The best form of government, like the most perfect of religions, taken in a literal sense, is a contradictory idea. The problem is not to discover how we shall be best governed, but how we shall be most free. Liberty commensurate and identical with Order,—this is the only reality of government and politics. How shall this absolute liberty, synonymous with order, be brought about? We shall be taught this by the analysis of the various formulas of authority. For all the rest we no more admit the governing of man by man than the exploitation of man by man." [16]

[56]

We have now climbed to the topmost heights of Proudhon's political philosophy. It is from this that the fresh and vivifying stream of his Anarchist thought flows. Before we follow the somewhat tortuous course of this stream let us glance back at the way we have climbed.

We fancied we were following Kant. We were mistaken. In his "Critique of Pure Reason" Kant has demonstrated the impossibility of proving the existence of God, because everything outside experience must escape us absolutely. In his "Critique of Practical Reason" Kant admitted the existence of God in the name of morality. But he has never declared that God was a topsy-turvy image of our own soul. What Proudhon attributes to Kant, indubitably belongs to Feuerbach. Thus it is in the footsteps of the [57] latter that we have been treading, while roughly tracing out the "biography" of the political Idea. So that Proudhon brings us back to the very starting point of our most unsentimental journey with Stirner. No matter. Let us once more return to the reasoning of Feuerbach.

It is only itself that humanity seeks in religion. It is only himself, it is liberty that the citizen seeks in Government. Then the very essence of the citizen is liberty? Let us assume this is true, but let us also note that our French "Kant" has done nothing, absolutely nothing, to prove the "legitimacy" of such an "Idea. " Nor is this all. What is this liberty which we are assuming to be the essence of the citizen? Is it political liberty which ought in the nature of things to be the main object of his attention? Not a bit of it! To assume this would be to make of the "citizen" an "authoritarian" democrat.

It is the *absolute liberty of the individual*, which is at the same time *commensurate and identical with* Order, that our citizen seeks in Government. In other words, it is the Anarchism of Proudhon which is the essence of the "citizen." It is impossible to make a more pleasing discovery, but the "biography" of this discovery gives us pause. We have been trying to demolish every argument in favour of the Idea of Authority, as Kant demolished every proof of the existence of God. To attain this end we have—imitating Feuerbach to some extent, according to whom man adored his own Being in God—assumed that it is liberty which [58] the citizen seeks in Government. And as to liberty we have in a trice transformed this into "absolute" liberty, into Anarchist liberty. Eins, zwei, drei; Geschwindigkeit ist keine Hexerei! [17]

Since the "citizen" only seeks "absolute" liberty in Government the State is nothing but a fiction ("this fiction of a superior person, called the 'State'"), and all those formulas of government for which people and citizens have been cutting one another's throats for the last sixty centuries, are but the "phantasmagoria of our brain, which it would be the first duty of free reason to relegate to the museums and libraries." Which is another charming discovery made *en passant*. So that the political history of humanity has, "for sixty centuries," had no other motive power than a phantasmagoria of our brain!

To say that man adores in God his own essence is to indicate the *origin* of religion, but it is not to work out its "biography." To write the biography of religion is to write its history, explaining the evolution of this essence of man which found expression in it. Feuerbach did not do this—could not do it. Proudhon, trying to imitate Feuerbach, was very far from recognising the insufficiency of his point of view. All Proudhon has done is to take Feuerbach for Kant, and to ape his Kant-Feuerbach in a most pitiful manner. Having heard that Divinity was but a fiction, he concluded that the State is also a figment: since God does not exist, how [59] can the State exist? Proudhon wished to combat the State and began by declaring it non-existent. And the readers of the "Voix du Peuple" applauded, and the opponents of M. Proudhon were alarmed at the profundity of his philosophy! Truly a tragi-comedy!

It is hardly necessary for modern readers to add that in taking the State for a fiction we make it altogether impossible to understand its "essence" or to explain its historical evolution. And this was what happened to Proudhon.

"In every society I distinguish two kinds of constitution," says he; "the one which I call *social*, the other which is its *political* constitution; the first innate in humanity, liberal, necessary, its development consisting above all in weakening, and gradually eliminating the second, which is essentially factitious, restrictive, and transitory. The social constitution is nothing but the equilibration of interests based upon free contract and the organisation of the economic forces, which, generally speaking, are labour, division of labour, collective force, competition, commerce, money, machinery, credit, property, equality in transactions, reciprocity of guarantees, etc. The principle of the political constitution is authority. Its forms are: distinction of classes, separation of powers, administrative centralisation, the judicial hierarchy, the representation of sovereignty by elections, etc. The political constitution was conceived and gradually completed in the interest of order, for want of a social constitution, the rules and principles of which could only be discovered as a result of [60] long experience, and are even to-day the object of Socialist controversy. These two constitutions, as it is easy to see, are by nature absolutely different and even incompatible: but as it is the fate of the political constitution to constantly call forth and produce the social constitution something of the latter enters into the former, which, soon becoming inadequate, appears contradictory and odious, is forced from concession to concession to its final abrogation." [18]

The social constitution is innate in humanity, necessary. Yet it could only be discovered as the result of long experience, and for want of it humanity had to invent the political constitution. Is not this an entirely Utopian conception of human nature, and of the social organisation peculiar to it? Are we not coming back to the standpoint of Morelly who said that humanity in the course of its history has always been "outside nature?" No—there is no need to come back to this standpoint, for with Proudhon we have never, for a single instant, got away from it. While looking down upon the Utopians searching after "the best form of government," Proudhon does not by any means censure the Utopian point of view. He only scoffs at the small perspicacity of men who did not divine that the best political organisation is the absence of all political organisation, is the social [61] organisation, proper to human nature, necessary, immanent in humanity.

The nature of this social constitution is absolutely different from, and even incompatible with, that of the political constitution. Nevertheless it is the fate of the political constitution to constantly call forth and produce the social constitution. This is tremendously confusing! Yet one might get out of the difficulty by assuming that what Proudhon meant to say was that the political constitutions act upon the evolution of the social constitution. But then we are inevitably met by the question. Is not the political constitution in its turn rooted—as even Guizot admitted—in the social constitution of a country? According to our author *no*; the more emphatically *no*, that the social organisation, the true and only one, is only a thing of the future, for want of which poor humanity has "invented" the political constitution. Moreover, the "Political Constitution" of Proudhon covers an immense domain, embracing even "class distinctions," and therefore "non-organised" property, property as it ought not to be, property as it is to-day. And since the whole of this political constitution has been invented as a mere stop-gap until the advent of the anarchist organisation of society, it is evident that all human history must have been one huge blunder. The State is no longer exactly a fiction as Proudhon maintained in 1848; "the governmental formulas" for which people and citizens have been cutting one another's throats for sixty centuries are no longer a "mere phantasmagoria of our [62] brain," as the same Proudhon believed at this same period; but these formulas, like the State itself, like every political constitution, are but the product of human ignorance, the mother of all fictions and phantasmagorias. At bottom it is always the same. The main point is that Anarchist ("social") organisation could only be discovered as the result of "many experiences." The reader will see how much this is to be regretted.

The political constitution has an unquestionable influence upon the social organisation; at any rate it calls it forth, for such is its "fate" as revealed by Proudhon, master of Kantian philosophy and social organisation. The most logical conclusion to be drawn therefrom is that the partisans of social organisation must make use of the political constitution in order to attain their end. But logical as this deduction is, it is not to the taste of our author. For him it is but a phantasmagoria of our brain. To make use of the political constitution is to offer a burnt offering to the terrible god of authority, to take part in the struggle of parties. Proudhon will have none of this. "No more parties," he says; "no more authority, absolute liberty of the man and the citizen—in three words, such is our political and social profession of faith." [19]

Every class-struggle is a political struggle. Whosoever repudiates the political struggle by this very act, gives up all part and lot in the [63] class-struggle. And so it was with Proudhon. From the beginning of the Revolution of 1848 he preached the reconciliation of classes. Here *e.g.*, is a passage from the Circular which he addressed to his electors in Doubs, which is dated 3rd April of this same year: "The social question is there; you cannot escape from it. To solve it we must have men who combine extreme Radicalism of mind with extreme Conservatism of mind. Workers, hold out your hands to your employers; and you, employers, do not deliberately repulse the advances of those who were your wage-earners."

The man whom Proudhon believed to combine this extreme Radicalism of mind with extreme Conservatism of mind, was himself—P. J. Proudhon. There was, on the one hand, at the bottom of this belief, a "fiction," common to all Utopians who imagine they can rise above classes and their struggles, and naïvely think that the whole of the future history of humanity will be confined to the peaceful propagation of their new gospel. On the other hand, this tendency to combine Radicalism and Conservatism shows conclusively the very "essence" of the "Father of Anarchy."

Proudhon was the most typical representative of petty bourgeois socialism. Now the "fate" of the petty bourgeois—in so far as he does not adopt the proletarian standpoint—is to constantly oscillate between Radicalism and Conservatism. To make more understandable what we have said, we must bear in mind what the [64] plan of social organisation propounded by Proudhon was.

Our author shall tell us himself. It goes without saying that we shall not escape a more or less authentic interpretation of Kant. "Thus the line we propose to follow in dealing with the political question and in preparing the materials for a constitution will be the same as that we have followed hitherto in dealing with the social question." The *Voix du Peuple* while completing the work of its predecessors, the two earlier journals, will follow faithfully in their footsteps. [20] What did we say in these two publications, one after the other of which fell beneath the blows of the reaction and the state of siege? We did not ask, as our precursors and colleagues had done, Which is the best system of community? The best organisation of property? Or again: Which is the better, property or the community? The theory of St. Simon or that of Fourier? The system of Louis Blanc or that of Cabet? Following the example of Kant we stated the question thus: "How is it that man possesses? How is property acquired? How lost? What is the law of its evolution and transformation? Whither does it tend? What does it want? What, in fine, does it represent?. Then how is it that man labours? How is the comparison of products instituted? By what means is circulation carried out in society? [65] Under what conditions? According to what laws?" And the conclusion arrived at by this monograph of property was this: Property indicates function or attribution; community; reciprocity of action; usury ever decreasing, the identity of labour and capital (*sic!*). In order to set free and to realise all these terms, until now hidden beneath the old symbols of property, what must be done? The workers must guarantee one another labour and a market; and to this end must accept as money their reciprocal pledges. Good! To-day we say that political liberty, like industrial liberty, will result for us from our mutual guarantees. It is by guaranteeing one another liberty that we shall get rid of this government, whose destiny is to symbolise the republican motto: *Liberty, Equality, Fraternity,* while leaving it to our intelligence to bring about the realisation of this. Now, what is the formula of this political and liberal guarantee? At present universal suffrage; later on free contract. Economic and social reform through the mutual guarantee of credit; political reform through the inter-action of individual liberties; such is the programme of the "*Voix du Peuple.*" [21] We may add to this that it is not very difficult to write the "biography" of this programme.

In a society of producers of commodities, the exchange of commodities is carried out according to the labour socially necessary for their production. Labour is the source and the [66] measure of their exchange-value. Nothing could seem more "just" than this to any man imbued with the ideas engendered by a society of producers of commodities. Unfortunately this "justice" is no more "eternal" than anything else here below. The development of the production of commodities necessarily brings in its train the transformation of the greater part of society into proletarians, possessing nothing but their labour-power, and of the other part into capitalists, who, buying this power, the only commodity of the proletarians, turn it into a source of wealth for themselves. In working for the capitalists the proletarian produces the income of his exploiter, at the same time as his own poverty, his own social subjection. Is not this sufficiently unjust? The partisan of the rights of the producer of commodities deplores the lot of the proletarians; he thunders against capital. But at the same time he thunders against the revolutionary tendencies of the proletarians who speak of expropriating the exploiter and of a communistic organisation of production. Communism is unjust, it is the most odious tyranny. What wants organising is not *production* but *exchange*, he assures us. But how organise exchange? That is easy enough, and what is daily going on before our eyes may serve to show us the way. Labour is the source and the measure of the *value* of commodities. But is the *price* of commodities always determined by their value? Do not prices continually vary according to the rarity or [67] abundance of these commodities? The value of a commodity and its price are two different things; and this is the misfortune, the great misfortune of all of us poor, honest folk, who only want justice, and only ask for our own. To solve the social question, therefore we must put a stop to the *arbitrariness of prices*, and to the anomaly of value (Proudhon's own expressions). And in order to do this we must "constitute" value; *i.e.*, see that every producer shall always, in exchange for his commodity, receive exactly what it costs. Then will private property not only cease to be theft, it will become the most adequate expression of justice. To constitute value is to constitute small private property, and small private property once constituted, everything will be justice and happiness in a world now so full of misery and injustice. And it is no good for proletarians to object, they have no means of production: by guaranteeing themselves *credit gratis*, all who want to work will, as by the touch of a magic wand, have everything necessary for production.

Small property and small parcelled-out production, its economic basis, was always the dream of Proudhon. The huge modern mechanical workshop always inspired him with profound aversion. He says that labour, like love, flies from society. No doubt there are some industries—Proudhon instances railways—in which *association* is essential. In these, the isolated producer must make way for "companies of workers." But the exception only proves the [68] rule. [22] Small private property must be the basis of "social organization."

Small private property is tending to disappear. The desire not merely to preserve it, but to transform it into the basis of a new social organisation is extreme conservatism. The desire at the same time to put an end to "the exploitation of man by man," to the wage-system, is assuredly to combine with the most conservative the most radical aspirations.

We have no desire here to criticise this petty bourgeois Utopia. This criticism has already been undertaken by a master hand in the works of Marx: "La Misère de la Philosophie," and "Zur Kritik der Politischen Oekonomie." We will only observe the following:—

The only bond that unites the producers of commodities upon the domain of economics is exchange. From the juridical point of view, exchange appears as the relation between two wills. The relation of these two wills is expressed in the "contract." The production of commodities duly "constituted" is therefore the reign of "absolute" individual liberty. By finding myself bound through a contract that obliges me to do such and such a thing, I do not renounce my liberty. I simply use it to enter into [69] relations with my neighbours. But at the same time this contract is the regulator of my liberty. In fulfilling a duty that I have freely laid upon myself when signing the contract, I render justice to the rights of others. It is thus that "absolute" liberty becomes "commensurate with order." Apply this conception of the contract to the "political constitution" and you have "Anarchy."

"The idea of the contract excludes that of government. What characterises the contract, reciprocal convention, is that by virtue of this convention the liberty and well-being of man are increased, while by the institution of authority both are necessarily decreased. Contract is thus essentially synallagmatic; it lays upon the contracting parties no other obligation than that which results from their personal promise of reciprocal pledges; it is subject to no external authority; it alone lays down a law common to both parties, and it can be carried out only through their own initiative. If the contract is already this in its most general acceptation and in its daily practice, what will the social contract be—that contract which is meant to bind together all the members of a nation by the same interest? The social contract is the supreme act by which every citizen pledges to society his love, his intellect, his labour, his service, his products, his possessions, in exchange for the affection, the ideas, the labour, products, service, and possessions of his fellows; the measure of right for each one being always determined by the extent of his own contribution, and [70] the amount recoverable being in accordance with what has been given. The social contract must be freely discussed, individually consented to, signed *manu propriâ*, by all who participate in it. If its discussion were prevented, curtailed or burked; if consent to it were filched; if the signature were given to a blank document in pure confidence, without a reading of the articles and their preliminary explanation; or even if, like the military oath, it were all predetermined and enforced, then the social contract would be nothing but a conspiracy against the liberty and well-being of the most ignorant, the most weak, and most numerous individuals, a systematic spoliation, against which every means of resistance or even of reprisal might become a right and a duty. The social contract is of the essence of the reciprocal contract; not only does it leave the signer the whole of his possessions; it adds to his property; it does not encroach upon his labour; it only affects exchange. Such, according to the definitions of right and universal practice, must be the social contract." [23]

Once it is admitted as an incontestable fundamental principle that the contract is "the only moral bond that can be accepted by free and equal human beings" nothing is easier than a "radical" criticism of the "political constitution." Suppose we have to do with justice and the penal law, for example? Well, Proudhon [71] would ask you by virtue of what contract society arrogates to itself the right to punish criminals. "Where there is no compact there can be, so far as any external tribunal is concerned, neither crime nor misdemeanour. The law is the expression of the sovereignty of the people; that is, or I am altogether mistaken, the social contract and the personal pledge of the man and the citizen. So long as I did not want this law, so long as I have not consented to it, voted for it, it is not binding upon me, it does not exist. To make it a precedent before I have recognised it, and to use it against me in spite of my protests is to make it retroactive, and to violate this very law itself. Every day you have to reverse a decision because of some formal error. But there is not a single one of your laws that is not tainted with nullity, and the most monstrous nullity of all, the very hypothesis of the law. Souffrard, Lacenaire, all the scoundrels whom you send to the scaffold turn in their graves and accuse you of judicial forgery. What answer can you make them?" [24]

If we are dealing with the administration and the police Proudhon sings the same song of contract and free consent. "Cannot we administer our goods, keep our accounts, arrange our differences, look after our common interests at least as well as we can look after our salvation and take care of our souls?" "What more have we to do with State legislation, with State [72] justice, with State police, and with State administration than with State religion?" [25]

As to the Ministry of Finance, "it is evident that its *raison d'être* is entirely included in that of the other ministries. Get rid of all the political harness and you will have no use for an administration whose sole object is the procuring and distribution of supplies." [26]

This is logical and "radical;" and the more radical, that this formula of Proudhon's—constituted value, free contract—is a universal one, easily, and even necessarily applicable to all peoples. "Political economy is, indeed, like all other sciences; it is of necessity the same all over the world; it does not depend upon the arrangements of men or nations, it is subject to no one's caprice. There is no more a Russian, English, Austrian, Tartar, or Hindoo political economy than there is a Hungarian, German, or American physics or geometry. Truth is everywhere equal to itself: Science is the unity of the human race. If science, therefore, and no longer religion or authority is taken in all countries as the rule of society, the sovereign arbiter of all interests, government becomes null and void, the legislators of the whole universe are in harmony." [27]

But enough of this! The "biography" of what Proudhon called his programme is now sufficiently clear to us. Economically it is but the Utopia of a petty bourgeois, who is firmly [73] convinced that the production of commodities is the most "just" of all possible modes of production, and who desires to eliminate its bad sides (hence his "Radicalism") by retaining to all eternity its good sides (hence his "Conservatism"). Politically the programme is only the application to public relations of a concept (the "contract") drawn from the domain of the private right of a society of producers of commodities. "Constituted value" in economics, the "contract" in politics—these are the whole scientific "truth" of Proudhon. It is all very well for him to combat the Utopians; he is a Utopian himself to his finger tips. What distinguishes him from men like Saint Simon, Fourier, and Robert Owen is his extreme pettiness and narrowness of mind, his hatred of every really revolutionary movement and idea.

Proudhon criticised the "political constitution" from the point of view of private right. He wished to perpetuate private property, and to destroy that pernicious "fiction" the State, for ever.

Guizot had already said that the political constitution of a country has its root in the conditions of property existing there. For Proudhon the political constitution owes its origin only to human ignorance, has only been "imagined" in default of the "social organisation" at last "invented" by him, Proudhon, in the year of our Lord so and so. He judges the political history of mankind like a Utopian. But the Utopian negation of all reality by no means preserves us from its influence. Denied upon one page of a [74] Utopian work, it takes its revenge on another, where it often appears in all its nakedness. Thus Proudhon "denies" the State. "The State—no, no—I will none of it, even as servant; I reject all government, even direct government," he cries *ad nauseam*. But, oh! irony of reality! Do you know how he "invents" the constitution of value? It is very funny.

The constitution of value is the selling at a fair price, at the cost price. [28] If a merchant refuses to supply his merchandise at cost price it is because he is not certain of selling a sufficient quantity to secure a due return, and further he has no guarantee that he will get *quid pro quo* for his purchases. So he must have guarantees. And there may be "various kinds" of these guarantees. Here is one.

"Let us suppose that the Provisional Government or the Constituent Assembly . had seriously wished to help along business, encourage commerce, industry, agriculture, stop the depreciation of property, assure work to the workers—it could have been done by guaranteeing, *e.g.*, to the first 10,000 contractors, factory owners, manufacturers, merchants, etc., in the whole Republic, an interest of 5 per cent. on the capital, say, on the average, 100,000 francs, that each of them had embarked in his competitive business. For it is evident that the State" . Enough! It is evident that the State has forced [75] itself upon Proudhon, at least "as servant." And it has done this with such irresistible force that our author ends by surrendering, and solemnly proclaiming:

"Yes, I say it aloud: the workers' associations of Paris and the departments hold in their hands the salvation of the people, the future of the revolution. They can do everything, if they set about it cleverly. Renewed energy on their part must carry the light into the dullest minds, and at the election of 1852 [he wrote this in the summer of 1851] must place on the order of the day, and at the head of it, the constitution of value." [29]

Thus "No more parties! No politics!" when it is a question of the class struggle—and "Hurrah for politics! Hurrah for electoral agitation! Hurrah for State interference!" when it is a question of realising the vapid and meagre Utopia of Proudhon!

"*Destruam et ædificabo*," says Proudhon, with the pompous vanity peculiar to him. But on the other hand—to use the phrase of Figaro—it is the truest truth of all he has ever uttered in his life. He destroys and he builds. Only the mystery of his "destruction" reveals itself completely in his formula, "The Contract solves all problems." The mystery of his "*ædificatio*" is in the strength of the social and political bourgeois reality with which he reconciled himself, the more readily in that he never managed to pluck from it any of its "secrets."

Proudhon will not hear of the State at any [76] price. And yet—apart from the political propositions such as the constitution of value, with which he turns to the odious "fiction"—even theoretically he "builds up" the State as fast as he "destroys" it. What he takes from the "State" he bestows upon the "communes" and "departments." In the place of one great State we see built up a number of small states; in the place of one great "fiction" a mass of little ones. To sum up, "anarchy" resolves itself into federalism, which among other advantages has that of making the success of revolutionary movements much more difficult than it is under a centralised State. [30] So endeth Proudhon's "General Idea of the Revolution."

It is a curious fact that Saint Simon is the "father" of Proudhon's anarchy. Saint Simon has said that the end of social organisation is production, and that, therefore, political science must be reduced to economics, the "art of governing men" must give way to the art of "administration of things." He has compared mankind to the individual, who, obeying his parents in childhood, in his ripe age ends by obeying no one but himself. Proudhon seized upon this idea and this comparison, and with the help of the constitution of value, "built up" anarchy. But Saint Simon, a man of fertile genius, would have been the very first to be alarmed at what this Socialistic petty bourgeois made of his theory. Modern scientific Socialism has worked out the theory of Saint Simon very differently, [77] and while explaining the historical origin of the State, shows in this very origin, the conditions of the future disappearance of the State.

"The State was the official representative of society as a whole, the gathering of it together into a visible embodiment. But it was this only in so far as it was the State of that class which itself represented, for the time being, society as a whole; in ancient times the State of slave-owning citizens; in the middle ages, the feudal lords; in our own time, the bourgeoisie. When at last it becomes the real representative of the whole of society, it renders itself unnecessary. As soon as there is no longer any social class to be held in subjection; as soon as class rule and the individual struggle for existence based on our present anarchy in production, with the collisions and excesses arising from these are removed, nothing more remains to be repressed, and a special repressive force, a State, is no longer necessary. The first act by virtue of which the State really constitutes itself the representative of the whole of society, the taking possession of the means of production in the name of society, this is, at the same time, its last independent act as a State. State interference in social relations becomes, in one domain after another, superfluous, and then dies out of itself; the government of persons is replaced by the administration of things, and by the conduct of processes of production. The State is not 'abolished.' *It dies out.* " [31]

FOOTNOTES:

[16] For all these quotations see the preface to the third edition of the "Confessions d'un Révolutionnaire." This preface is simply an article reprinted from the *Voix du Peuple*, November, 1849. It was not till 1849 that Proudhon began to "expound" his Anarchist theory. In 1848, *pace* Kropotkine, he only expounded his theory of exchange, as anyone can see for himself by reading the sixth volume of his complete works (Paris, 1868). This "critique" of Democracy, written in March, 1848, did not yet expound his Anarchist theory. This "critique" forms part of his work, "Solution du Problème Social," and Proudhon proposes to bring about this solution "without taxes, without loans, without cash payments, without paper-money, without maximum, without levies, without bankruptcy, without agrarian laws, without any poor tax, without national workshops, without association (!), without any participation or intervention by the State, without any interference with the liberty of commerce and of industry, without any violation of property," in a word and above all, without any class war. A truly "immortal" idea and worthy the admiration of all bourgeois, peace-loving, sentimental, or bloodthirsty—white, blue, or red!

[17] "One, two, three; legerdemain isn't witchcraft."

[18] "Les Confessions d'un Révolutionnaire." Vol. ix., 1868 edition of the complete works of Proudhon, pages 166 and 167.

[19] "Confessions," pp. 25-26.

[20] He is speaking of the two papers *Le Peuple* and *Le Réprésentant du Peuple*, which he had published in 1848-9 before the *Voix du Peuple*.

[21] "Confessions," pp. 7-8.

[22] For Proudhon the principle of association invoked by most schools (he means the various Socialist schools), "a principle essentially sterile, is neither an industrial force nor an economic law . it supposes government and obedience, two terms excluded by the Revolution." (*Idée Générale de la Révolution au XIX Siècle*, 2 ed., Paris 1851, p. 173).

[23] "Idée Générale de la Revolution. " Paris, 1851, pp. 124-127.

[24] "Idée Générale," pp. 298-299.

[25] "Idée Générale," p. 304.

[26] Ibid. p. 324.

[27] Ibid. p. 328.

[28] It was thus that Proudhon understood the determining of value by labour. He could never understand a Ricardo.

[29] "Idée Générale," p. 268.

[30] See his book, "Du Principe Fédératif."

[31] *Socialism: Utopian and Scientific.* By F. Engels. Translated by Edward Aveling. Pp. 75-77.

[78]

CHAPTER V

BAKOUNINE

We have seen that in their criticism of the "political constitution," the "fathers" of anarchy always based themselves on the Utopian point of view. Each one of them based his theories upon an abstract principle. Stirner upon that of the "Ego," Proudhon upon that of the "Contract." The reader has also seen that these two "fathers" were individualists of the first water.

The influence of Proudhonian individualism was, for a time, very strong in the Romance countries (France, Belgium, Italy, Spain) and in the Slaav countries, especially Russia. The internal history of the International Working Men's Association is the history of this struggle between Proudhonism and the modern Socialism of Marx. Not only men like Tolain, Chemalé or Murat, but men very superior to them, such as De Paepe, *e.g.*, were nothing but more or less opinionated, more or less consistent "Mutualists." But the more the working class movement developed, the more evident it became that "Mutualism" could not be its theoretical expression. At the International Congresses the Mutualists were forced by the logic [79] of facts to vote for the Communist resolutions. This was the case, *e.g.*, at Brussels in the discussion on landed property. [32] Little by little the left wing of the Proudhonian army left the domain of Individualism to intrench itself upon that of "Collectivism."

The word "Collectivism" was used at this period in a sense altogether opposed to that which it now has in the mouths of the French Marxists, like Jules Guesde and his friends. The most prominent champion of "Collectivism" was at this time Michel Bakounine.

[80]

In speaking of this man we shall pass over in silence his propaganda in favour of the Hegelian philosophy, as far as he understood it, the part he played in the revolutionary movement of 1848, his Panslavist writings in the beginning of the sixties, and his pamphlet, "Roumanow, Pougatchew or Pestel" [33] (London, 1862), in which he proposed to go over to Alexander II., if the latter would become the "Tzar of the Moujiks." Here we are exclusively concerned with his theory of Anarchist Collectivism.

A member of the "League of Peace and Liberty," Bakounine, at the Congress of this Association at Berne in 1869, called upon the League—an entirely bourgeois body—to declare in favour of "the economical and social equalisation of classes and of individuals." Other delegates, among whom was Chaudey, reproached him with advocating Communism. He indignantly protested against the accusation.

"Because I demand the economic and social equalisation of classes and individuals, because, with the Workers' Congress of Brussels, I have declared myself in favour of collective property, I have been reproached with being a Communist. What difference, I have been asked, is there [81] between Communism and Collectivism. I am really astounded that M. Chaudey does not understand this difference, he who is the testamentary executor of Proudhon! I detest Communism, because it is the negation of liberty, and I cannot conceive anything human without liberty. I am not a Communist, because Communism concentrates and causes all the forces of society to be absorbed by the State, because it necessarily ends in the centralisation of property in the hands of the State, while I desire the abolition of the State—the radical extirpation of this principle of the authority and the tutelage of the State, which, under the prbook of moralising and civilising men, has until now enslaved, oppressed, exploited, and depraved them. I desire the organisation of society and of collective or social property from below upwards, by means of free association, and not from above downwards by means of some authority of some sort. Desiring the abolition of the State, I desire the abolition of property individually hereditary, which is nothing but an institution of the State, nothing but a result of the principle of the State. This is the sense, gentlemen, in which I am a Collectivist, and not at all a Communist."

In another speech at the same Congress Bakounine reiterates what he had already said of "Statist" Communism. "It is not we, gentlemen," he said, "who systematically deny all authority and all tutelary powers, and who in the name of Liberty demand the very abolition of the "authoritarian" principle of the State; it is not we who will recognise any sort of political [82] and social organisation whatever, that is not founded upon the most complete liberty of every one. But I am in favour of collective property, because I am convinced that so long as property, individually hereditary, exists, the equality of the first start, the realisation of equality, economical and social, will be impossible." [34] This is not particularly lucid as a statement of principles. But it is sufficiently significant from the "biographical" point of view.

We do not insist upon the ineptitude of the expression "the economic and social equalisation of classes;" the General Council of the International dealt with that long ago. [35] We would only remark that the above quotations show that Bakounine—

1. Combats the State and "Communism" in the name of "the most complete liberty of everybody;"

2. Combats property, "individually hereditary," in the name of economic equality;

3. Regards this property as "an institution of [83] the State," as a "consequence of the very principles of the State;"

4. Has no objection to individual property, if it is not hereditary; has no objection to the right of inheritance, if it is not individual.

In other words:

1. Bakounine is quite at one with Proudhon so far as concerns the negation of the State and Communism;

2. To this negation he adds another, that of property, individually hereditary;

3. His programme is nothing but a total arrived at by the adding up of the two abstract principles—that of "liberty," and that of "equality;" he applies these two principles, one after the other, and independently one of the other, in his criticism of the existing order of things, never asking himself whether the results of these two negations are reconcilable with one another.

4. He understands, just as little as Proudhon, the origin of private property and the causal connection between its evolution and the development of political forms.

5. He has no clear conception of the meaning of the words "individually hereditary."

If Proudhon was a Utopian, Bakounine was doubly so, for his programme was nothing but a Utopia of "Liberty," reinforced by a Utopia of "Equality." If Proudhon, at least to a very large extent, remained faithful to his principle of the contract, Bakounine, divided between liberty and equality, is obliged from the very outset of his argument constantly to throw over the [84] former for the benefit of the latter, and the latter for the benefit of the former. If Proudhon is a Proudhonian *sans reproche*, Bakounine is a Proudhonian adulterated with "detestable" Communism, nay even by "Marxism."

In fact, Bakounine has no longer that immutable faith in the genius of the "master" Proudhon, which Tolain seems to have preserved intact. According to Bakounine "Proudhon, in spite of all his efforts to get a foothold upon the firm ground of reality, remained an idealist and metaphysician. His starting point is the abstract side of law; it is from this that he starts in order to arrive at economic facts, while Marx, on the contrary, has enunciated and proved the truth, demonstrated by the whole of the ancient and modern history of human societies, of peoples and of states, that economic facts preceded and precede the facts of political and civil law. The discovery and demonstration of this truth is one of the greatest merits of M. Marx." [36] In another of his writings he says, with entire conviction, "All the religions, and all the systems of morals that govern a given society are always the ideal expression of its real, material condition, that is, especially of its economic organisation, but also of its political organisation, the latter, indeed, being never anything but the juridical and violent consecration [85] of the former." And he again mentions Marx as the man to whom belongs the merit of having discovered and demonstrated this truth. [37] One asks oneself with astonishment how this same Bakounine could declare that private property was only a consequence of the principle of authority. The solution of the riddle lies in the fact that he did not understand the materialist conception of history; he was only "adulterated" by it.

And here is a striking proof of this. In the Russian work, already quoted, "Statism and Anarchy," he says that in the situation of the Russian people there are two elements which constitute the conditions necessary for the social (he means Socialist) revolution. "The Russian people can boast of excessive poverty, and unparalleled slavery. Their sufferings are innumerable, and they bear these, not with patience, but with a profound and passionate despair, that twice already in our history has manifested itself in terrible outbursts: in the revolt of Stephan Razine, and in that of Pougatschew." [38] And that is what Bakounine understood by the material conditions of a Socialist revolution! Is it necessary to point out that this "Marxism" is a little too *sui generis*?

While combating Mazzini from the standpoint of the materialist conception of history, Bakounine himself is so far from understanding the true [86] import of this conception, that in the same work in which he refutes the Mazzinian theology, he speaks, like the thorough-faced Proudhonian that he is, of "absolute" human morality, and he bolsters up the idea of this morality—the morality of "solidarity,"—with such arguments as these:

"Every actual being, so long as he exists, exists only by virtue of a principle which is inherent in himself, and which determines his particular nature; a principle that is not imposed upon him by a divine law-giver of any sort" (this is the "materialism" of our author!), "but is the protracted and constant result of combinations of natural causes and effects; that is not, according to the ludicrous idea of the idealists, shut up in him like a soul within its body, but is, in fact, only the inevitable and constant form of his real existence. The human, like all other species, has inherent principles quite special to itself, and all these principles are summed up in, or are reducible to, a single principle, which we call *solidarity*. This principle may be formulated thus: No human individual can recognise his own humanity, nor, therefore, realise it in his life except by recognising it in others, and by helping to realise it for others. No man can emancipate himself, except by emancipating with him all the men around him. My liberty is the liberty of everyone, for I am not truly free, free not only in thought but in deed, except when my liberty and my rights find their confirmation, their [87] sanction, in the liberty and the rights of all men, my equals." [39]

As a moral precept, solidarity, as interpreted by Bakounine, is a very excellent thing. But to set up this a morality, which by the way is not at all "absolute," as principle "inherent" in humanity and determining human nature, is playing with words, and completely ignoring what materialism is. Humanity only exists "by virtue" of the principle of solidarity. This is coming it a little too strong. How about the "class war," and the cursed State, and property, "individually hereditary"—are these only manifestations of "solidarity," inherent in humanity, determining its special nature, etc., etc? If this is so, everything is all right, and Bakounine was wasting his time in dreaming of a "social" revolution. If this is not so, this proves that humanity may have existed "by virtue" of other principles than that of solidarity, and that this latter principle is by no means "inherent" in it. Indeed, Bakounine only enunciated his "absolute" principle in order to arrive at the conclusion that "no people could be completely free, free with solidarity, in the human sense of the word, if the whole of humanity is not free also." [40]

This is an allusion to the tactics of the modern proletariat, and it is true in the sense that—as the rules of the International Workingmen's Association put it—the emancipation of the workers is not a merely local or national problem, [88] but, on the contrary, a problem concerning every civilised nation, its solution being necessarily dependent upon their theoretical and practical co-operation. It is easy enough to prove this truth by reference to the actual economic situation of civilised humanity. But nothing is less conclusive, here as elsewhere, than a "demonstration" founded upon a Utopian conception of "human nature." The "solidarity" of Bakounine only proves that he remained an incorrigible Utopian, although he became acquainted with the historical theory of Marx.

FOOTNOTES:

[32] " . Among those who call themselves Mutualists, and whose economic ideas incline, on the whole, to the theories of Proudhon, in the sense that they, like the great revolutionary writer, demand the suppression of all levies of capital upon labour, the suppression of interest, reciprocity of service, equal exchange of products on the basis of cost price, free reciprocal credit, several voted for the collective ownership of the land. Such, *e.g.*, are the four French delegates, Aubry of Rouen, Delacour of Paris, Richard of Lyons, Lemonnier of Marseilles, and among the Belgians, Companions A. Moetens, Verricken, De Paepe, Marichal, etc. For them there is no contradiction between Mutualism applicable to the exchange of services and the exchange of products on the basis of cost price, that is to say, the quantity of labour contained in the services and the products, and collective property applicable to the land, which is not a product of labour, and therefore does not seem to them to come under the law of exchange, under the law of circulation."—Reply to an article by Dr. Coullery in the "Voix de l'Avenir," September, 1868, by the Belgians Vanderhouten, De Paepe, Delasalle, Hermann, Delplanque, Roulants, Guillaume Brasseur, printed in the same newspaper and reprinted as a document in the "Mémoire of the Fédération Jurasienne," Souvillier, 1873, pp. 19-20.

[33] "Roumanow" is the name of the reigning family in Russia—derived (if we overlook the adultery of Catherine II., admitted by herself in her memoirs) from Peter III., the husband of Catherine II., and Prince of Holstein-Gottorp. Pougatchew, the pretended Peter III., was a Cossack, who placed himself at the head of a Russian peasant rising in 1773. Pestel was a Republican conspirator, hanged by Nicolas in 1826.

[34] See the documents published with the "Mémoire de la Fédération Jurasienne," pp. 28, 29, 37.

[35] "The equalisation of classes," wrote the General Council to the "Alliance" of Bakounine, who desired to be admitted into the International Working Men's Association, and had sent the Council its programme in which this famous "equalisation" phrase occurs, "literally interpreted comes to the harmony of capital and labour, so pertinaciously advocated by bourgeois Socialists. It is not the equalisation of classes, logically a contradiction, impossible to realise, but on the contrary, the abolition of classes, the real secret of the proletarian movement, which is the great aim of the International Working Men's Association."

[36] "Statism and Anarchy, 1873" (the Russian place of publication is not given), pp. 223-224 (Russian). We know the word "Statism" is a barbarism, but Bakounine uses it, and the flexibility of the Russian language lends itself to such forms.

[37] "La Théologie Politique de Mazzini et l'Internationale, Neuchatel, 1871," pp. 69 and 78.

[38] Ibid. Appendix A, p. 7.

[39] "La Théologié Politique de Mazzini," p. 91.

[40] Ibid. pp. 110, 111.

[89]

CHAPTER VI

BAKOUNINE—(CONCLUDED)

We have said that the principal features of Bakounine's programme originated in the simple addition of two abstract principles: that of liberty and that of equality. We now see that the total thus obtained might easily be increased by the addition of a third principle, that of solidarity. Indeed, the programme of the famous "Alliance," adds several others. For example, "The Alliance declares itself Atheist; it desires the abolition of religions, the substitution of science for faith, of human for divine justice." In the proclamation with which the Bakounists placarded the walls of Lyons, during the attempted rising at the end of September, 1870, we read (Article 41) that "The State, fallen into decay, will no longer be able to intervene in the payment of private debts." This is incontestably logical, but it would be difficult to deduce the non-payment of private debts from principles inherent in human nature.

Since Bakounine in tacking his various "absolute" principles together does not ask himself, and does not need to ask himself—thanks to the "absolute" character of his method—whether one of these principles might not somewhat limit [90] the "absolute" power of others, and might not in its turn be limited by them, he finds it an "absolute" impossibility to harmonise the various items of his programme whenever words no longer suffice, and it becomes necessary to replace them by more precise ideas. He "desires" the abolition of religion. But, "the State having fallen into decay," who is to abolish it? He "desires" the abolition of property, individually hereditary. But what is to be done if, "the State having fallen into decay," it should continue to exist? Bakounine himself feels the thing is not very clear, but he consoles himself very easily.

In a pamphlet written during the Franco-German war, "Lettres à un français sur la crise actuelle," while demonstrating that France can only be saved by a great revolutionary movement, he comes to the conclusion that the peasants must be incited to lay hands upon the land belonging to the aristocracy and the bourgeoisie. But so far, the French peasants have been in favour of property, "individually hereditary," so this unpleasant institution would be bolstered up by the new Social Revolution?

"Not at all," answers Bakounine, "*once the State is abolished they*" (*i. e.*, the peasants) "*will no longer have the juridical and political consecration, the guarantee of property by the State. Property will no longer be a right, it will be reduced to the condition of a simple fact.*" (The italics are Bakounine's own.)

This is very reassuring. "The State having fallen into decay," any fellow that happens to [91] come along, stronger than I, will incontinently possess himself of my field, without having any need to appeal to the principal of "solidarity;" the principle of "liberty" will sufficiently answer his purpose. A very pleasant "equalisation of individuals"!

"It is certain," Bakounine admits, "that at first things won't work in an absolutely peaceful manner; there will be struggles; public order, that arch saint of the bourgeois, will be disturbed, and the just deeds which will result from such a state of things may constitute what one is agreed to call a civil war. But do you prefer to hand over France to the Prussians?. Moreover, do you fear that the peasants will devour one another; even if they tried to do so in the beginning, they would soon be convinced of the material impossibility of persisting in this course, and then we may be sure they would try to arrive at some understanding, to come to terms, to organise among themselves. The necessity of eating, of providing for their families, and the necessity therefore of safeguarding their houses, their families, and their own lives against unforeseen attacks, all this would soon force them individually to enter into mutual arrangements. And do not believe, either, that in these arrangements, *arrived at outside all official tutelage*" (italicised by Bakounine), "by the mere force of events, the strongest, the richest, will exercise a predominant influence. The wealth of the wealthy, no longer guaranteed by juridical institutions, will cease to be a power. As to the most cunning, [92] the strongest, they will be rendered innocuous by the collective strength of the mass of the small, and very small peasants, as well as by the agricultural proletarians, a mass of men to-day reduced to silent suffering, but whom the revolutionary movement will arm with an irresistible power. Please note that I do not contend that the agricultural districts which will thus reorganise themselves, from below upwards, will immediately create an ideal organisation, agreeing at all points with the one of which we dream. What I am convinced of is that this will be a *living* organisation, and as such, one a thousand times superior to what exists now. Moreover, this new organisation being always open to the propaganda of the towns, as it can no longer be held down, so to say petrified by the juridical sanction of the State, it will progress freely, developing and perfecting itself indefinitely, but always living and free, never decreed nor legalised, until it attains as reasonable a condition as we can hope for in our days."

The "idealist" Proudhon was convinced that the political constitution had been invented for want of a social organisation "immanent in humanity." He took the pains to "discover" this latter, and having discovered it, he could not see what further *raison d'être* there was for the political constitution. The "materialist" Bakounine has no "social organisation" of his own make. "The most profound and rational science," he says, "cannot divine the future forms [93] of social life." [41] This science must be content to distinguish the "living" social forms from those that owe their origin to the "petrifying" action of the State, and to condemn these latter. Is not this the old Proudhonian antithesis of the social organisation "immanent in humanity," and of the political constitution "invented" exclusively in the interests of "order?" Is not the only difference that the "materialist" transforms the Utopian programme of the "idealist," into something even more Utopian, more nebulous, more absurd?

"To believe that the marvellous scheme of the universe is due to chance, is to imagine that by throwing about a sufficient number of printers' characters at hazard, we might write the Iliad." So reasoned the Deists of the 18th century in refuting the Atheists. The latter replied that in this case everything was a question of time, and that by throwing about the letters an infinite number of times, we must certainly, at some period, make them arrange themselves in the required sequence. Discussions of this kind were to the taste of the 18th century, and we should be wrong to make too much fun of them now-a-days. But it would seem that Bakounine took the Atheist argument of the good old [94] times quite seriously, and used it in order to make himself a "programme." Destroy what exists; if only you do this often enough you are bound at last to produce a social organisation, approaching at any rate the organisation you "dream" of. All will go well when once the revolution has come to stay. Is not this sufficiently "materialist?" If you think it is not, you are a metaphysician, "dreaming" of the impossible!

The Proudhonian antithesis of the "social organisation" and the "political constitution" reappears "living" and in its entirety in what Bakounine is for ever reiterating as to the "social revolution" on the one hand, and the "political revolution" on the other. According to Proudhon the social organisation has unfortunately, up to our own days, never existed, and for want of it humanity was driven to "invent" a political constitution. According to Bakounine the social revolution has never yet been made, because humanity, for want of a good "social" programme had to content itself with political revolutions. Now that this programme has been found, there is no need to bother about the "political" revolution; we have quite enough to do with the "social revolution."

Every class struggle being necessarily a political struggle, it is evident that every political revolution, worthy of the name, is a social revolution; it is evident also that for the proletariat the political struggle is as much a necessity as it has always been for every class struggling to emancipate itself. Bakounine anathematises all [95] political action by the proletariat; he extols the "social" struggle exclusively. Now what is this social struggle?

Here our Proudhonian once again shows himself adulterated by Marxism. He relies as far as possible upon the Rules of the International Workingmen's Association.

In the preamble of these Rules it is laid down that the subjection of the worker to capital lies at the bottom of all servitude, political, moral and material, and that therefore the economic emancipation of the workers is the great end to which all political movements must be subordinated as a means. Bakounine argues from this that "every political movement which has not for its immediate and direct object the final and complete economic emancipation of the workers, and which has not inscribed upon its banner quite definitely and clearly, the principle of *economic equality*, that is, the integral restitution of capital to labour, or else the social liquidation—every such political movement is a bourgeois one, and as such must be excluded from the International." But this same Bakounine has heard it said that the historical movement of humanity is a process in conformity with certain laws, and that a revolution cannot be improvised at a moment's notice. He is therefore forced to ask himself, what is the policy which the International is to adopt during that "more or less prolonged period of time which separates us from the terrible social revolution which everyone foresees today?" To this he replies, with the most profound [96] conviction, and, as if quoting the Rules of the International:

"Without mercy the policy of the democratic bourgeois, or bourgeois-Socialists, must be excluded, which, when these declare that political freedom is a necessary condition of economic emancipation, can only mean this: political reforms, or political revolutions must precede economic reforms or economic revolutions; the workers must therefore join hands with the more or less Radical bourgeois, in order to carry out the former together with them, then, being free, to turn the latter into a reality against them. We protest loudly against this unfortunate theory, which, so far as the workers are concerned, can only result in their again letting themselves be used as tools against themselves, and handing them over once more to bourgeois exploitation."

The International "commands" us to disregard all national or local politics; it must give the working-class movement in all countries an "essentially economic" character, by setting up as final aim "the shortening of the hours of labour, and the increase of wages," and as a means "the association of the working masses, and the starting of funds for fighting." It is needless to add that the shortening of the hours of labour must, of course, be obtained without any intervention from the accursed State. [42]

Bakounine cannot understand that the [97] working class in its political action can completely separate itself from all the exploiting parties. According to him, there is no other *rôle* in the political movement for the workers than that of satellite of the Radical bourgeoisie. He glorifies the "essentially economic" tactics of the old English Trade Unions, and has not the faintest idea that it was these very tactics that made the English workers the tail of the Liberal Party.

Bakounine objects to the working class lending a hand in any movement whose object is the obtaining or the extension of political rights. In condemning such movements as "bourgeois," he fancies himself a tremendous revolutionist. As a matter of fact he thus proves himself essentially Conservative, and if the working class were ever to follow this line of inaction the Governments could only rejoice. [43]

The true revolutionists of our days have a very different idea of Socialist tactics. They "everywhere support every revolutionary movement against the existing social and political order of things;" [44] which does not prevent them (but quite the contrary) from forming the proletariat into a party separate from all the exploiter parties, opposed to the whole "reactionary mass."

Proudhon, who we know had not any overwhelming sympathy for "politics," nevertheless advised the French workers to vote for the [98] candidates who pledged themselves to "constitute value." Bakounine would not have politics at any price. The worker cannot make use of political liberty: "in order to do so he needs two little things—leisure and material means." So it is all only a bourgeois lie. Those who speak of working-class candidates are but mocking the proletariat. "Working-class candidates, transferred to bourgeois conditions of life, and into an atmosphere of completely bourgeois political ideas, ceasing to be actually workers in order to become statesmen, will become bourgeois, and possibly will become even more bourgeois than the bourgeois themselves. For it is not the men who make positions, but, on the contrary, positions which make the men." [45]

This last argument is about all Bakounine was able to assimilate of the materialist conception of history. It is unquestionably true that man is the product of his social environment. But to apply this incontestable truth with advantage it is necessary to get rid of the old, metaphysical method of thought which considers things *one after the other, and independently one of the other*. Now Bakounine, like his master, Proudhon, in spite of his flirtation with the Hegelian philosophy, all his life remained a metaphysician. He does not understand that the environment which makes man may change, thus changing man its own product. The environment he has in his mind's eye when speaking of the political action of the proletariat, is the bourgeois [99] parliamentary environment, that environment which must necessarily fatally corrupt labour representatives. But the environment of the *electors*, the environment of a working-class party, conscious of its aim and well organised, would this have no influence upon the elected of the proletariat? No! Economically enslaved, the working class must always remain in political servitude; in this domain it will always be the weakest; to free itself it must begin by an economic revolution. Bakounine does not see that by this process of reasoning he inevitably arrives at the conclusion that a victory of the proletariat is absolutely impossible, unless the owners of the means of production voluntarily relinquish their possessions to them. In effect the subjection of the worker to capital is the source not only of political but of moral servitude. And how can the workers, morally enslaved, rise against the bourgeoisie? For the working class movement to become possible, according to Bakounine, it must therefore first make an economic revolution. But the economic revolution is only possible as the work of the workers themselves. So we find ourselves in a vicious circle, out of which modern Socialism can easily break, but in which Bakounine and the Bakounists are for ever turning with no other hope of deliverance than a logical *salto mortale*.

The corrupting influence of the Parliamentary environment on working-class representatives is what the Anarchists have up to the present considered the strongest argument in their criticism [100] of the political activity of Social-Democracy. We have seen what its *theoretical* value amounts to. And even a slight knowledge of the history of the German Socialist party will sufficiently show how in practical life the Anarchist apprehensions are answered.

In repudiating all "politics" Bakounine was forced to adopt the tactics of the old English Trade Unions. But even he felt that these tactics were not very revolutionary. He tried to get out of the difficulty by the help of his "Alliance," a kind of international secret society, organised on a basis of frenetic centralisation and grotesque fancifulness. Subjected to the dictatorial rule of the sovereign pontiff of Anarchy, the "international" and the "national" brethren were bound to accelerate and direct the "essentially economic" revolutionary movement. At the same time Bakounine approved of "riots," of isolated risings of workers and peasants which, although they must inevitably be crushed out, would, he declared, always have a good influence upon the development of the revolutionary spirit among the oppressed. It goes without saying that with such a "programme" he was able to do much harm to the working class movement, but he was not able to draw nearer, even by a single step, to that "immediate" economic revolution of which he "dreamed." [46] We shall presently see the result [101] of the Bakounist theory of "riots." For the present let us sum up what we have said of Bakounine. And here, he shall help us himself.

"Upon the Pangermanic banner" [*i.e.*, also upon the banner of German Social-Democracy, and consequently upon the Socialist banner of the whole civilised world] "is inscribed: The conservation and strengthening of the State at all costs; on the Socialist-revolutionary banner" (read Bakounist banner) "is inscribed in characters of blood, in letters of fire: the abolition of all States, the destruction of bourgeois civilisation; free organisation from the bottom to the top, by the help of free associations; the organisation of the working populace (*sic!*) freed from all trammels, the organisation of the whole of emancipated humanity, the creation of a new human world."

It is with these words that Bakounine concludes his principal work "Statism and Anarchy" (Russian). We leave our readers to appreciate the rhetorical beauties of this passage. For our own part we shall be content with saying that it contains absolutely no human meaning whatsoever.

The absurd, pure and simple—that is what is inscribed upon the Bakounist "banner." There is no need of letters of fire and of blood to make this evident to any one who is not hypnotised [102] by a phraseology more or less sonorous, but always void of sense.

The Anarchism of Stirner and of Proudhon was completely individualist. Bakounine did not want individualism, or to speak more correctly, one particular phase of individualism. He was the inventor of "Collectivist-Anarchism." And the invention cost him little. He completed the "liberty" Utopia, by the "equality" Utopia. As these two Utopias would not agree, as they cried out at being yoked together, he threw both into the furnace of the "permanent revolution" where they were both at last forced to hold their tongues, for the simple reason that they both evaporated, the one as completely as the other.

Bakounine is the *décadent* of Utopism.

FOOTNOTES:

[41] "Statism and Anarchy," Appendix A. But for Russia the "science" of Bakounine was quite equal to divining the future forms of social life; there is to be the Commune, whose ulterior development will start from the actual rural commune. It was especially the Bakounists who in Russia spread the notion about the marvellous virtues of the Russian rural commune.

[42] See Bakounine's articles on the "Politics of the International" in the *Egalité* of Geneva, August, 1869.

[43] The anathemas pronounced by Bakounine against political liberty for a time had a very deplorable influence upon the revolutionary movement in Russia.

[44] Communist Manifesto, p. 30.

[45] *Egalité*, 28th August, 1869.

[46] On the action of Bakounine in the International, see the two works published by the General Council of that organisation: *Les Prétendus Scissions dans l'Internationale*, and *L'Alliance de la Democratic Sociale*. See also Engels' article *Die Bakunisten an der Arbeit*, reprinted in the recently published pamphlet, *Internationales aus dem Volkstaat* (*i.e.*, a series of articles published in the *Volkstaat*,) 1873-75. Berlin, 1894.
[103]

CHAPTER VII

THE SMALLER FRY

Among our present-day Anarchists some, like John Mackay, the author of "Die Anarchisten, Kulturgemälde aus dem Ende des xix. Jahrhunderts," declare for individualism, while others—by far the more numerous—call themselves Communists. These are the descendants of Bakounine in the Anarchist movement. They have produced a fairly considerable literature in various languages, and it is they who are making so much noise with the help of the "propaganda by deed." The prophet of this school is the Russian refugee, P. A. Kropotkine.

I shall not here stop to consider the doctrines of the Individualist-Anarchist of to-day, whom even their brethren, the Communist-Anarchists, look upon as "bourgeois." [47] We will go straight on to the Anarchist-"Communist."

[104]

What is the standpoint of this new species of Communism? "As to the method followed by the Anarchist thinker, it entirely differs from that of the Utopists," Kropotkine assures us. "The Anarchist thinker does not resort to metaphysical conceptions (like 'natural rights,' the 'duties of the State' and so on) to establish what are, in his opinion, the best conditions for realising the greatest happiness of humanity. He follows, on the contrary, the course traced by the modern philosophy of evolution. He studies human society as it is now, and was in the past; and, without either endowing men altogether, or separate individuals, with superior qualities which they do not possess, he merely considers society as an aggregation of organisms trying to find out the best ways of combining the wants of the individual with those of cooperation for the welfare of the species. He studies society and tries to discover its tendencies, past and present, its growing needs, intellectual and economical, and in this he merely points out in which direction evolution goes." [48]

So the Anarchist-Communists have nothing in common with the Utopians. They do not, in the elaborating of their "ideal," turn to [105] metaphysical conceptions like "natural rights," the "duties of the State," etc. Is this really so?

So far as the "duties of the State" are concerned, Kropotkine is quite right; it would be too absurd if the Anarchists invited the State to disappear in the name of its own "duties." But as to "natural rights" he is altogether mistaken. A few quotations will suffice to prove this.

Already in the *Bulletin de la Fédération Jurasienne* (No. 3, 1877), we find the following very significant declaration: "The sovereignty of the people can only exist through the most complete autonomy of individuals and of groups." This "most complete autonomy," is it not also a "metaphysical conception?"

The *Bulletin de la Fédération Jurasienne* was an organ of Collectivist Anarchism. At bottom there is no difference between "Collectivist" and "Communist" Anarchism. And yet, since it might be that we are making the Communists responsible for the Collectivists, let us glance at the "Communist" publications, not only according to the spirit but the letter. In the autumn of 1892 a few "companions" appeared before the Assize Court of Versailles in consequence of a theft of dynamite at Soisy-sous-Etiolles. Among others there was one G. Etiévant, who drew up a declaration of Anarchist-Communist principles. The tribunal would not allow him to read it, whereupon the official organ of the Anarchists, *La Révolte*, undertook to publish this declaration, having taken great pains to secure an absolutely correct copy of the [106] original. The "Declaration of G. Etiévant" made a sensation in the Anarchist world, and even "cultured" men like Octave Mirbeau quote it with respect along with the works of the "theorists," Bakounine, Kropotkine, the "unequalled Proudhon," and the "aristocratic Spencer!" Now this is the line of Etiévant's reasoning:

No idea is innate in us; each idea is born of infinitely diverse and multiple sensations, which we receive by means of our organs. Every act of the individual is the result of one or several ideas. The man is not therefore responsible. In order that responsibility should exist, will would have to determine the sensations, just as these determine the idea, and the idea, the act. But as it is, on the contrary, the sensations which determine the will, all judgment becomes impossible, every reward, every punishment unjust, however great the good or the evil done may be. "Thus one cannot judge men and acts unless one has a sufficient criterion. Now no such criterion exists. At any rate it is not in the laws that it could be found, for true justice is immutable and laws are changeable. It is with laws as with all the rest (!). For if laws are beneficent what is the good of deputies and senators to change them? And if they are bad what is the good of magistrates to apply them?"

Having thus "demonstrated" "liberty," Etiévant passes on to "equality."

From the zoophytes to men, all beings are provided with more or less perfect organs destined to serve them. All these beings have [107] therefore the right to make use of their organs according to the evident will of mother Nature. "So for our legs we have the right to all the space they can traverse; for our lungs to all the air we can breathe; for our stomach to all the food we can digest; for our brain to all we can think, or assimilate of the thoughts of others; for our faculty of elocution to all we can say; for our ears to all we can hear; and we have a right to all this because we have a right to life, and because all this constitutes life. These are the true rights of man! No need to decree them, they exist as the sun exists. They are written in no constitution, in no law, but they are inscribed in ineffaceable letters in the great book of Nature and are imprescriptible. From the cheese-mite to the elephant, from the blade of grass to the oak, from the atom to the star, everything proclaims it."

If these are not "metaphysical conceptions," and of the very worst type, a miserable caricature of the metaphysical materialism of the eighteenth century, if this is the "philosophy of evolution," then we must confess that it has nothing in common with the scientific movement of our day.

Let us hear another authority, and quote the now famous book of Jean Grave, "La Société mourante et l'Anarchie," which was recently condemned by French judges, who thought it dangerous, while it is only supremely ridiculous.

"Anarchy means the negation of authority. Now, Government claims to base the legitimacy of its existence upon the necessity of defending [108] social institutions: the family, religion, property, etc. It has created a vast machinery in order to assure its exercise and its sanction. The chief are: the law, the magistracy, the army, the legislature, executive powers, etc. So that the Anarchist idea, forced to reply to everything, was obliged to attack all social prejudices, to become thoroughly penetrated by all human knowledge, in order to demonstrate that its conceptions were in harmony with the physiological and psychological nature of man, and in harmony with the observance of natural laws, while our actual organisation has been established in contravention of all logic and all good sense. Thus, in combating authority, it has been necessary for the Anarchists to attack all the institutions which the Government defends, the necessity for which it tries to demonstrate in order to legitimate its own existence." [49]

You see what was "the development" of the "Anarchist Idea." This Idea "denied" authority. In order to defend itself, authority appealed to the family, religion, property. Then the "Idea" found itself forced to attack institutions, which it had not, apparently, noticed before, and at the same time the "Idea," in order to make the most of its "conceptions," penetrated to the very depths of all human knowledge (it is an ill wind that does not blow some good!) All this is only the result of chance, of the unexpected turn given by "authority" to [109] the discussion that had arisen between itself and the "Idea."

It seems to us that however rich in human knowledge it may be now, the "Anarchist Idea" is not at all communistic; it keeps its knowledge to itself, and leaves the poor "companions" in complete ignorance. It is all very well for Kropotkine to sing the praises of the "Anarchist thinker"; he will never be able to prove that his friend Grave has been able to rise even a little above the feeblest metaphysics.

Kropotkine should read over again the Anarchist pamphlets of Elisée Reclus—a great "theorist" this—and then, quite seriously tell us if he finds anything else in them but appeals to "justice," "liberty," and other "metaphysical conceptions."

Finally, Kropotkine himself is not so emancipated from metaphysics as he fancies he is. Far from it! Here, *e.g.*, is what he said at the general meeting of the Federation of the Jura, on the 12th October, 1879, at Chaux-de-Fonds:—

"There was a time when they denied Anarchists even the right to existence. The General Council of the International treated us as factious, the press as dreamers; almost all treated us as fools; this time is past. The Anarchist party has proved its *vitality*; it has surmounted the obstacles of every kind that impeded its development; to-day it is *accepted*." [By whom?] "To attain to this, it has been necessary, above all else, for the party to hold its own in the domain of *theory*, to establish its ideal of the society of the future, to prove that this ideal is [110] the best; to do more than this—to prove that this ideal is not the product of the dreams of the study, but flows directly from the popular aspirations, that it is in accord with the historical progress of culture and ideas. This work has been done," etc.

This hunt after the best ideal of the society of the future, is not this the Utopian method *par excellence*? It is true that Kropotkine tries to prove "that this ideal is not the product of dreams of the study, but flows directly from the popular aspirations, that it is in accord with the historical progress of culture and ideas." But what Utopian has not tried to prove this equally with himself? Everything depends upon the value of the proofs, and here our amiable compatriot is infinitely weaker than the great Utopians whom he treats as metaphysicians, while he himself has not the least notion of the actual methods of modern social science. But before examining the value of these "proofs," let us make the acquaintance of the "ideal" itself. What is Kropotkine's conception of Anarchist society?

Pre-occupied with the reorganising of the governmental machine, the revolutionist-politicians, the "Jacobins" (Kropotkine detests the Jacobins even more than our amiable Empress, Catherine II., detested them) allowed the people to die of hunger. The Anarchists will act differently. They will destroy the State, and will urge on the people to the expropriation of the rich. Once this expropriation accomplished, an "inventory" of the common wealth will be [111] made, and the "distribution" of it organised. Everything will be done by the people themselves. "Just give the people elbow room, and in a week the business of the food supply will proceed with admirable regularity. Only one who has never seen the hard-working people at their labour, only one who has buried himself in documents, could doubt this. Speak of the organising capacity of the Great Misunderstood, the People, to those who have seen them at Paris on the days of the barricades" (which is certainly not the case of Kropotkine) "or in London at the time of the last great strike, when they had to feed half a million starving people, and they will tell you how superior the people is to all the hide-bound officials." [50]

The basis upon which the enjoyment in common of the food supply is to be organised will be very fair, and not at all "Jacobin." There is but one, and only one, which is consistent with sentiments of justice, and is really practical. The taking in heaps from what one possesses abundance of! Rationing out what must be measured, divided! Out of 350 millions who inhabit Europe, 200 millions still follow this perfectly natural practice—which proves, among other things, that the Anarchist ideal "flows from the popular aspirations."

It is the same with regard to housing and clothing. The people will organise everything according to the same rule. There will be an upheaval; that is certain. Only this upheaval [112] must not become mere loss, it must be reduced to a minimum. And it is again—we cannot repeat it too often—by turning to those immediately interested and not to bureaucrats that the "least amount of inconvenience will be inflicted upon everybody." [51]

Thus from the beginning of the revolution we shall have an *organisation*; the whims of sovereign "individuals" will be kept within reasonable bounds by the wants of society, by the logic of the situation. And, nevertheless, we shall be in the midst of full-blown Anarchy; individual liberty will be safe and sound. This seems incredible, but it is true; there is anarchy, and there is organisation, there are obligatory rules for everyone, and yet everyone does what he likes. You do not follow. 'Tis simple enough. This organisation—it is not the "authoritarian" revolutionists who will have created it;—these rules, obligatory upon all, and yet anarchical, it is the People, the Great Misunderstood, who will have proclaimed them, and the People are very knowing as anyone who has seen,—what Kropotkine never had the opportunity of seeing—days of barricade riots, knows. [52]

But if the Great Misunderstood had the [113] stupidity to create the "bureaux" so detested of Kropotkine? If, as it did in March, 1871, it gave itself a revolutionary Government? Then we shall say the people is mistaken, and shall try to bring it back to a better state of mind, and if need be we will throw a few bombs at the "hide bound officials." We will call upon the People to organise, and will destroy all the organs it may provide itself with.

This then is the way in which we realise the excellent Anarchist ideal—in imagination. In the name of the liberty of individuals all action of the individuals is done away with, and in the name of the People we get rid of the whole class of revolutionists; the individuals are drowned in the mass. If you can only get used to this logical process, you meet with no more [114] difficulties, and you can boast that you are neither "authoritarian" nor "Utopian." What could be easier, what more pleasant?

But in order to consume, it is necessary to produce. Kropotkine knows this so well that he reads the "authoritarian" Marx a lesson on the subject.

"The evil of the present organisation is not in that the 'surplus value' of production passes over to the capitalist—as Rodbertus and Marx had contended—thus narrowing down the Socialist conception, and the general ideas on the capitalist regime. Surplus value itself is only a consequence of more profound causes. The evil is that there can be any kind of 'surplus value,' instead of a surplus not consumed by each generation; for, in order that there may be 'surplus value,' men, women, and children must be obliged by hunger to sell their labour powers, for a trifling portion of what these powers produce, and, especially of what they are capable of producing" (poor Marx, who knew nothing of all these profound truths, although so confusedly expounded by the learned Prince!). "It does not, indeed, suffice to distribute in equal shares the profits realised in one industry, if, at the same time, one has to exploit thousands of other workers. The point is to *produce with the smallest possible expenditure of human labour power the greatest possible amount of products necessary for the well being of all*." (Italicised by Kropotkine himself.)

Ignorant Marxists that we are! We have never heard that a Socialist society pre-supposes [115] a systematic organisation of production. Since it is Kropotkine who reveals this to us, it is only reasonable that we should turn to him to know what this organisation will be like. On this subject also he has some very interesting things to say.

"Imagine a Society comprising several million inhabitants engaged in agriculture, and a great variety of industries—Paris, for example, with the Department of Seine-et-Oise. Imagine that in this Society all children learn to work with their hand as well as with their brain. Admit, in fine, that all adults, with the exception of the women occupied with the education of children, undertake to work *five hours a day* from the age of twenty or twenty-two to forty-five or fifty, and that they spend this time in any occupations they choose, in no matter what branch of human labour considered *necessary*. Such a Society could, in return, guarantee well-being to all its members, *i.e.*, far greater comfort than that enjoyed by the bourgeoisie to-day. And every worker in this Society would moreover have at his disposal at least five hours a day, which he could devote to science, to art, and to those individual needs that do not come within the category of *necessities*, while later on, when the productive forces of man have augmented, everything may be introduced into this category that is still to-day looked upon as a luxury or unattainable." [53]

In Anarchist Society there will be no [116] authority, but there will be the *Contract* (oh! immortal Monsieur Proudhon, here you are again; we see all still goes well with you!) by virtue of which the infinitely free individuals "agree" to work in such or such a "free commune." The contract is justice, liberty, equality; it is Proudhon, Kropotkine, and all the Saints. But, at the same time, do not trifle with the contract! It is a thing not so destitute of means to defend itself as would seem. Indeed, suppose the signatory of a contract freely made does not wish to fulfil his duty? He is driven forth from the free commune, and he runs the risk of dying of hunger—which is not a particularly gay outlook.

"I suppose a group or a certain number of volunteers, combining in some enterprise, to secure the success of which all rival each other in zeal, with the exception of one associate, who frequently absents himself from his post. Should they, on his account, dissolve the group, appoint a president who would inflict fines, or else, like the Academy, distribute attendance-counters? It is evident that we shall do neither the one nor the other, but that one day the comrade who threatens to jeopardise the enterprise will be told: 'My friend, we should have been glad to work with you, but as you are often absent from your post, or do your work negligently, we must part. Go and look for other comrades who will put up with your off-hand ways.'" [54] This is pretty strong at bottom; but note how appearances are saved, how very [117] "Anarchist" is his language. Really, we should not be at all surprised if in the "Anarchist-Communist" society people were guillotined by persuasion, or, at any rate, by virtue of a freely-made contract.

But farther, this very Anarchist method of dealing with lazy "free individuals" is perfectly "natural," and "is practised everywhere to-day in all industries, in competition with every possible system of fines, stoppages from wages, espionage, etc.; the workman may go to his shop at the regular hour, but if he does his work badly, if he interferes with his comrades by his laziness or other faults, if they fall out, it is all over. He is obliged to leave the workshop." [55] Thus is the Anarchist "Ideal" in complete harmony with the "tendencies" of capitalist society.

For the rest, such strong measures as these will be extremely rare. Delivered from the yoke of the State and capitalist exploitation, individuals will of their own free motion set themselves to supply the wants of the great All of society. Everything will be done by means of "free arrangement."

"Well, Citizens, let others preach industrial barracks, and the convent of "Authoritarian" Communism, we declare that the *tendency* of societies is in the opposite direction. We see millions and millions of groups constituting themselves freely in order to satisfy all the varied wants of human beings, groups formed, some by [118] districts, by streets, by houses; others holding out hands across the walls (!) of cities, of frontiers, of oceans. All made up of human beings freely seeking one another, and having done their work as producers, associating themselves, to consume, or to produce articles of luxury, or to turn science into a new direction. This is the tendency of the nineteenth century, and we are following it; we ask only to develop it freely, without let or hindrance on the part of governments. Liberty for the individual!" "Take some pebbles," said Fourier, "put them into a box and shake them; they will arrange themselves into a mosaic such as you could never succeed in producing if you told off some one to arrange them harmoniously." [56]

A wit has said that the profession of faith of the Anarchists reduces itself to two articles of a fantastic law: (1) There shall be nothing. (2) No one is charged with carrying out the above article.

This is not correct. The Anarchists say:

(1) There shall be everything. (2) No one is held responsible for seeing that there is anything at all.

This is a very seductive "Ideal," but its realisation is unfortunately very improbable.

Let us now ask, what is this "free agreement" which according to Kropotkine, exists even in capitalist society? He quotes two kinds of examples by way of evidence: (*a*) those [119] connected with production and the circulation of commodities; (*b*) those belonging to all kinds of societies of amateurs—learned societies, philanthropic societies, etc.

"Take all the great enterprises: the Suez Canal, *e.g.*, Trans-Atlantic navigation, the telegraph that unites the two Americas. Take, in fine, this organisation of commerce, which provides that when you get up in the morning you are sure to find bread at the bakers' . meat at the butchers', and everything you want in the shops. Is this the work of the State? Certainly, to-day we pay middlemen abominably dearly. Well, all the more reason to suppress them, but not to think it necessary to confide to the Government the care of providing our goods and our clothing." [57]

Remarkable fact! we began by snapping our fingers at Marx, who only thought of suppressing surplus value, and had no idea of the organisation of production, and we end by demanding the suppression of the profits of the middleman, while, so far as production is concerned, we preach the most bourgeois *laissez-faire, laissez passer*. Marx might, not without reason, have said, he laughs best who laughs last!

We all know what the "free agreement" of the bourgeois *entrepreneur* is, and we can only admire the "absolute" naïveté of the man who sees in it the precursor of communism. It is exactly this Anarchic "arrangement" that must [120] be got rid of in order that the producers may cease to be the slaves of their own products. [58]

As to the really free societies of *savants*, artists, philanthropists, etc., Kropotkine himself tells us what their example is worth. They are "made up of human beings freely seeking one another after having done their work as producers." Although this is not correct—since in these societies there is often not a single *producer*—this still farther proves that we can only be free after we have settled our account with production. The famous "tendency of the nineteenth century," therefore, tells us nothing on the main question—how the unlimited liberty of the individual can be made to harmonise with the economic requirements of a communistic society. And as this "tendency" constitutes the whole of the scientific equipment of our "Anarchist thinker," we are driven to the conclusion that his appeal to science was merely verbiage, that he is, in spite of his contempt for the Utopians, one of the least ingenious of these, a vulgar hunter in search of the "best Ideal."

The "free agreement" works wonders, if not in Anarchist society, which unfortunately does not yet exist, at least in Anarchist arguments. "Our present society being abolished, individuals no longer needing to hoard in order to make sure of the morrow, this, indeed being made impossible, by the suppression of all money or symbol of value—all their wants being satisfied and [121] provided for in the new society, the stimulus of individuals being now only that ideal of always striving towards the best, the relations of individuals or groups no longer being established with a view to those exchanges in which each contracting party only seeks to 'do' his partner" (the "free agreement" of the bourgeois, of which Kropotkine has just spoken to us) "these relations will now only have for object the rendering of mutual services, with which particular interests have nothing to do, the agreement will be rendered easy, the causes of discord having disappeared." [59]

Question: How will the new society satisfy the needs of its members? How will it make them certain of the morrow?

Answer: By means of free agreements.

Question: Will production be possible if it depends solely upon the free agreement of individuals?

Answer: Of course! And in order to convince yourself of it, you have only to *assume* that your morrow is certain, that all your needs are satisfied, and, in a word, that production, thanks to free agreement, is getting on swimmingly.

What wonderful logicians these "companions" are, and what a beautiful ideal is that which has no other foundation than an illogical assumption!

"It has been objected that in leaving [122] individuals free to organise as they like, there would arise that competition between groups which to-day exists between individuals. This is a mistake, for in the society we desire money would be abolished, consequently there would no longer be any exchange of products, but exchange of services. Besides, in order that such a social revolution as we contemplate can have been accomplished we must assume that a certain evolution of ideas will have taken place in the mind of the masses, or, at the least, of a considerable minority among them. But if the workers have been sufficiently intelligent to destroy bourgeois exploitation, it will not be in order to re-establish it among themselves, especially when they are assured all their wants will be supplied." [60]

It is incredible, but it is incontestably true: the only basis for the "Ideal" of the Anarchist-Communists, is this *petitio principii*, this "assumption" of the very thing that has to be proved. Companion Grave, the "profound thinker," is particularly rich in assumptions. As soon as any difficult problem presents itself, he "assumes" that it is already solved, and then everything is for the best in the best of ideals.

The "profound" Grave is less circumspect than the "learned" Kropotkine. And so it is only he who succeeds in reducing the "ideal" to "absolute" absurdity.

He asks himself what will be done if in "the society of the day after the revolution" there should be a papa who should refuse his child [123] *all education*. The papa is an individual with unlimited rights. He follows the Anarchist rule, "Do as thou wouldst." No one has any right, therefore, to bring him to his senses. On the other hand, the child also may do as he likes, and he wants to learn. How to get out of this conflict, how resolve the dilemma without offending the holy laws of Anarchy? By an "assumption." "Relations" (between citizens) "being much wider and more imbued with fraternity than in our present society, based as it is upon the antagonism of interests, it follows that the child by means of what he will see passing before his eyes, by what he will daily hear, will escape from the influence of the parent, and will find every facility necessary for acquiring the knowledge his parents refuse to give him. Nay more, if he finds himself too unhappy under the authority they try to force upon him, he would abandon them in order to place himself under the protection of individuals with whom he was in greater sympathy. The parents could not send the gendarmes after him to bring back to their authority the slave whom the law to-day gives up to them." [61]

It is not the child who is running away from his parents, but the Utopian who is running away from an insurmountable logical difficulty. And yet this judgment of Solomon has seemed so profound to the companions that, it has been literally quoted by Emil Darnaud in his book "La Société Future" (Foix. 1890, p. 26)—a book [124] especially intended to popularise the lucubrations of Grave.

"Anarchy, the No-government system of Socialism, has a double origin. It is an outgrowth of the two great movements of thought in the economical and the political fields which characterise our century, and especially its second part. In common with all Socialists, the Anarchists hold that the private ownership of land, capital, and machinery has had its time; that it is condemned to disappear; and that all requisites of production must, and will, become the common property of society, and be managed in common by the producers of wealth. And, in common with the most advanced representatives of political Radicalism, they maintain that the ideal of the political organisation of society is a condition of things where the functions of government are reduced to a minimum, and the individual recovers his full liberty of initiative and action for satisfying, by means of free groups and federations—freely constituted—all the infinitely varied needs of the human being. As regards Socialism, most of the Anarchists arrive at its ultimate conclusion, that is, at a complete negation of the wage-system, and at Communism. And with reference to political organisation, by giving a farther development to the above-mentioned part of the Radical programme, they arrive at the conclusion that the ultimate aim of society is the reduction of the functions of governments to *nil*—that is, to a society without government, to Anarchy. The Anarchists maintain, moreover, that such being the ideal of social [125] and political organisation they must not remit it to future centuries, but that only those changes in our social organisation which are in accordance with the above double ideal, and constitute an approach to it, will have a chance of life and be beneficial for the commonwealth." [62]

Kropotkine here reveals to us, with admirable clearness, the origin and nature of his "Ideal." This Ideal, like that of Bakounine, is truly "double;" it is really born of the connection between bourgeois Radicalism, or rather that of the Manchester school, and Communism; just as Jesus was born in connection between the Holy Ghost and the Virgin Mary. The two natures of the Anarchist ideal are as difficult to reconcile as the two natures of the Son of God. But one of these natures evidently gets the better of the other. The Anarchists "want" to begin by immediately realising what Kropotkine calls "the ultimate aim of society," that is to say, by destroying the "State." Their starting point is always the unlimited liberty of the individual. Manchesterism before everything. Communism only comes in afterwards. [63] But in order to reassure us as to the probable fate of this second [126] nature of their Ideal, the Anarchists are constantly singing the praises of the wisdom, the goodness, the forethought of the man of the "future." He will be so perfect that he will no doubt be able to organise Communist production. He will be so perfect that one asks oneself, while admiring him, why he cannot be trusted with a little "authority."

FOOTNOTES:

[47] The few Individualists we come across are only strong in their criticism of the State and of the law. As to their constructive ideal, a few preach an idyll that they themselves would never care to practise, while others, like the editor of *Liberty*, Boston, fall back upon an ac-

tual bourgeois system. In order to defend their Individualism they reconstruct the State with all its attributes (law, police, and the rest) after having so courageously denied them. Others, finally, like Auberon Herbert, are stranded in a "Liberty and Property Defence League"—a League for the defence of landed property. *La Révolte*, No. 38, 1893, "A lecture on Anarchism."

[48] "Anarchist-Communism; its Basis and Principles," by Peter Kropotkine, republished by permission of the Editor of the *Nineteenth Century*. February and August, 1887, London.

[49] *l.c.*, pp. 1-2.

[50] "La Conquête du Pain." Paris, 1892. pp. 77-78.

[51] Ibid., p. 111.

[52] As, however, Kropotkine was in London at the time of the great Dock Strike, and therefore had an opportunity of learning how the food supply was managed for the strikers, it is worth pointing out that this was managed quite differently from the method suggested above. An organised Committee, consisting of Trade Unionists helped by State Socialists (Champion) and Social-Democrats (John Burns, Tom Mann, Eleanor Marx Aveling, etc.) made *contracts* with shopkeepers, and distributed stamped tickets, for which could be obtained certain articles of food. The food supplied was paid for with the money that had been raised by subscriptions, and to these subscriptions the *bourgeois* public, encouraged by the *bourgeois* press, had very largely contributed. Direct distributions of food to strikers, and those thrown out of work through the strike, were made by the Salvation Army, an essentially centralised, bureaucratically organised body, and other philanthropic societies. All this has very little to do with the procuring and distributing of the food supply, "the day after the revolution;" with the organising of the "service for supplying food." The food was there, and it was only a question of buying and dividing it as a means of support. The "People," *i.e.*, the strikers, by no means helped themselves in this respect; they were helped by others.

[53] "La Conquête du Pain," pp. 128-129.

[54] Ibid., pp. 201-202.

[55] Ibid., p. 202.

[56] "*L'Anarchie dans l'Evolution socialiste.*" Lecture at the Salle Levis, Paris, 1888, pp. 20-21.

[57] Ibid., p. 19.

[58] Kropotkine speaks of the Suez Canal! Why not the Panama Canal?

[59] "La Société au lendemain de la Révolution." J. Grave, 1889, Paris, pp. 61-62.

[60] Ibid., p. 47.

[61] Ibid., p. 99.

[62] Anarchist Communism, p. 3.

[63] "L'Anarchia è il funzionamento armonico di tutte le autonomie, risolventesi nella eguaglianza totale delle condizioni umane." L'Anarchia nella scienza e nelle evoluzione. (Traduzione dello Spagnuolo) Piato, Toscana, 1892, p. 26. "Anarchy is the harmonious functioning of all autonomy resolved in the complete equalisation of all human conditions." "Anarchy in Science and Evolution."—Italian, translated from the Spanish.

[127]

CHAPTER VIII

THE SO-CALLED ANARCHIST TACTICS. THEIR MORALITY

The Anarchists are Utopians. Their point of view has nothing in common with that of modern scientific Socialism. But there are Utopias and Utopias. The great Utopians of the first half of our century were men of genius; they helped forward social science, which in their time was still entirely Utopian. The Utopians of to-day, the Anarchists, are the abstracters of quintessence, who can only fully draw forth some poor conclusions from certain mummified principles. They have nothing to do with social science, which, in its onward march, has distanced them by at least half a century. Their "profound thinkers," their "lofty theorists," do not even succeed in making the two ends of their reasoning meet. They are the decadent Utopians, stricken with incurable intellectual anæmia. The great Utopians did much for the development of the working class movement. The Utopians of our days do nothing but retard its progress. And it is especially their so-called tactics that are harmful to the proletariat.

We already know that Bakounine interpreted the Rules of the International in the sense that [128] the working class must give up all political action, and concentrate its efforts upon the domain of the "immediately economic" struggle for higher wages, a reduction of the hours of labour, and so forth. Bakounine himself felt that such tactics were not very revolutionary. He tried to complete them through the action of his "Alliance;" he preached riots. [64] But the more the class consciousness of the proletariat develops, the more it inclines towards political action, and gives up the "riots," so common during its infancy. It is more difficult to induce the working men of Western Europe, who have attained a certain degree of political development, to riot, than, for example, the credulous and ignorant Russian peasants. As the proletariat has shown no taste for the tactics of "riot," the companions have been forced to replace it by "individual action." It was especially after the attempted insurrection at Benevento in Italy in 1877 that the Bakounists began to glorify the "propaganda of deed." But if we glance back at the period that separates us from the attempt of Benevento, we shall see that this propaganda too assumed a special form: very few "riots," and these quite insignificant, a great many personal attempts against public edifices, against individuals, and even against [129] property—"individually hereditary," of course. It could not be otherwise.

"We have already seen numerous revolts by people who wished to obtain urgent reforms," says Louise Michel, in an interview with a correspondent of the *Matin*, on the occasion of the Vaillant attempt. "What was the result? The people were shot down. Well, we think the people has been sufficiently bled; it is better large-hearted people should sacrifice themselves, and, at their own risk, commit acts of violence whose object is to terrorise the Government and the bourgeois." [65]

This is exactly what we have said—only in slightly different words. Louise Michel has forgotten to say that revolts, causing the bloodshed of the people, figured at the head of the Anarchists' programme, until the Anarchists became convinced, not that these partial risings in no way serve the cause of the workers, but that the workers, for the most part, will not have anything to do with these risings.

Error has its logic as well as truth. Once you reject the political action of the working-class, you are fatally driven—provided you do not wish to serve the bourgeois politicians—to accept the tactics of the Vaillants and the Henrys. The so-called "Independent" (Unabhängige) members of the German Socialist Party have proved this in their own persons. They began by attacking "Parliamentarism," and to the [130] "reformist" tactics of the "old" members they opposed—on paper, of course—the "revolutionary struggle," the purely "economic" struggle. But this struggle, developing naturally, must inevitably bring about the entry of the proletariat into the arena of political struggles. Not wishing to come back to the very starting-point of their negation, the "Independents," for a time, preached what they called "political demonstrations," a new kind of old Bakounist riots. As riots, by whatever name they are called, always come too late for the fiery "revolutionists," there was only left to the Independents to "march forward," to become converts to Anarchy, and to propagate—in words—the propaganda of deed. The language of the "young" Landauers and Co. is already as "revolutionary" as that of the "oldest" Anarchists.

"Reason and knowledge only thou despise
The highest strength in man that lies!
Let but the lying spirit bind thee,
With magic works and shows that blind thee,
And I shall have thee fast and sure."

As to the "magic work and shows," they are innumerable in the arguments of the Anarchists against the political activity of the proletariat. Here hate becomes veritable witchcraft. Thus Kropotkine turns their own arm—the materialist conception of history—against the Social-Democrats. "To each new economical phase of life corresponds a new political phase," he assures us. "Absolute monarchy—that is Court-rule—corresponded to the system of serfdom. [131] Representative government corresponds to capital-rule. Both, however, are class-rule. But in a society where the distinction between capitalist and labourer has disappeared, there is no need of such a government; it would be an anachronism, a nuisance." [66] If Social-Democrats were to tell him they know this at least as well as he does, Kropotkine would reply that possibly they do, but that then they will not draw a logical conclusion from these premises. He, Kropotkine, is your real logician. Since the political constitution of every country is determined by its economic condition, he argues, the political action of Socialists is absolute nonsense. "To seek to attain Socialism or even (!) an agrarian revolution by means of a political revolution, is the merest Utopia, because the whole of history shows us that political changes flow from the great economic revolutions, and not *vice versâ*." [67] Could the best geometrician in the world ever produce anything more exact than this demonstration? Basing his argument upon this impregnable foundation, Kropotkine advises the Russian revolutionists to give up their political struggle against Tzarism. They must follow an "immediately economic" end. "The emancipation of the Russian peasants from the yoke of serfdom that has until now weighed upon them, is therefore the first task of the Russian revolutionist. In working along these lines he directly and immediately [132] works for the good of the people . and he moreover prepares for the weakening of the centralised power of the State and for its limitation." [68]

Thus the emancipation of the peasants will have prepared the way for the weakening of Russian Tzarism. But how to emancipate the peasants before overthrowing Tzarism? Absolute mystery! Such an emancipation would be a veritable "witchcraft." Old Liscow was right when he said, "It is easier and more natural to write with the fingers than with the head."

However this may be, the whole political action of the working-class must be summed up in these few words: "No politics! Long live the purely economic struggle!" This is Bakounism, but perfected Bakounism. Bakounine himself urged the workers to fight for a reduction of the hours of labour, and higher wages. The Anarchist-Communists of our day seek to "make the workers understand that they have nothing to gain from such child's play as this, and that society can only be transformed by destroying the institutions which govern it." [69] The raising of wages is also useless. "North America and South America, are they not there to prove to us that whenever the worker has succeeded in getting higher wages, the prices of articles of consumption have increased proportionately, and that where he has succeeded in getting 20 francs a [133] day for his wages, he needs 25 to be able to live according to the standard of the better class workman, so that he is always below the average?" [70] The reduction of the hours of labour is at any rate superfluous since capital will always make it up by a "systematic intensification of labour by means of improved machinery. Marx himself has demonstrated this as clearly as possible." [71]

We know, thanks to Kropotkine, that the Anarchist ideal has a double origin. And all the Anarchist "demonstrations" also have a double origin. On the one hand they are drawn from the vulgar hand books of political economy, written by the most vulgar of bourgeois economists, *e.g.*, Grave's dissertation upon wages, which Bastiat would have applauded enthusiastically. On the other hand, the "companions," remembering the somewhat "Communist" origin of their ideal, turn to Marx and quote, without understanding, him. Even Bakounine has been "sophisticated" by

Marxism. The latter-day Anarchists, with Kropotkine at their head, have been even more sophisticated.

The ignorance of Grave, "the profound thinker," is very remarkable in general, but it exceeds the bounds of all probability in matters of political economy. Here it is, only equalled by that of the learned geologist Kropotkine, who makes the most monstrous statements whenever he touches upon an economic question. We regret [134] that space will not allow us to amuse the reader with some samples of Anarchist economics. They must content themselves with what Kropotkine has taught them about Marx's "surplus-value."

All this would be very ridiculous, if it were not too sad, as the Russian poet Lermontoff says. And it is sad indeed. Whenever the proletariat makes an attempt to somewhat ameliorate its economic position, "large-hearted people," vowing they love the proletariat most tenderly, rush in from all points of the compass, and depending on their halting syllogisms, put spokes into the wheel of the movement, do their utmost to prove that the movement is useless. We have had an example of this with regard to the eight hours day, which the Anarchists combated, whenever they could, with a zeal worthy of a better cause. When the proletariat takes no notice of this, and pursues its "immediately economic" aims undisturbed—as it has the fortunate habit of doing—the same "large-hearted people" re-appear upon the scene armed with bombs, and provide the government with the desired and sought for prbook for attacking the proletariat. We have seen this at Paris on May 1, 1890; we have seen it often during strikes. Fine fellows these "large-hearted men!" And to think that among the workers themselves there are men simple enough to consider as their friends, these personages who are, in reality, the most dangerous enemies of their cause!

An Anarchist will have nothing to do with "parliamentarism," since it only lulls the proletariat to sleep. He will none of "reforms," since [135] reforms are but so many compromises with the possessing classes. He wants the revolution, a "full, complete, immediate, and immediately economic" revolution. To attain this end he arms himself with a saucepan full of explosive materials, and throws it amongst the public in a theatre or a café. He declares this is the "revolution." For our own part it seems to us nothing but "immediate" madness.

It goes without saying that the bourgeois governments, whilst inveighing against the authors of these attempts, cannot but congratulate themselves upon these tactics. "Society is in danger!" *Caveant consules!* And the police "consuls" become active, and public opinion applauds all the reactionary measures resorted to by ministers in order to "save society." "The terrorist saviours of society in uniform, to gain the respect of the Philistine masses must appear with the halo of true sons of 'holy order,' the daughter of Heaven rich in blessings, and to this halo the schoolboy attempts of these Terrorists help them. Such a silly fool, lost in his fantastical imaginings, does not even see that he is only a puppet, whose strings are pulled by a cleverer one in the Terrorist wings; he does not see that the fear and terror he causes only serve to so deaden all the senses of the Philistine crowd, that it shouts approval of every massacre that clears the road for reaction." [72]

Napoleon III. already indulged from time to time in an "outrage" in order once again to save [136] society menaced by the enemies of order. The foul admissions of Andrieux, [73] the acts and deeds of the German and Austrian *agents provocateurs*, the recent revelations as to the attempt against the Madrid Parliament, etc., prove abundantly that the present Governments profit enormously by the tactics of the "companions," and that the work of the Terrorists in uniform would be much more difficult if the Anarchists were not so eager to help in it.

Thus it is that spies of the vilest kind, like Joseph Peukert, for long years figured as shining lights of Anarchism, translating into German the works of foreign Anarchists; thus it is that the French bourgeois and priests directly subvention [137] the "companions," and that the law-and-order ministry does everything in its power to throw a veil over these shady machinations. And so, too, in the name of the "immediate revolution," the Anarchists become the precious pillars of bourgeois society, inasmuch as they furnish the *raison d'être* for the most immediately reactionary policy.

Thus the reactionary and Conservative press has always shown a hardly disguised sympathy for the Anarchists, and has regretted that the Socialists, conscious of their end and aim, will have nothing to do with them. "They drive them away like poor dogs," pitifully exclaims the Paris *Figaro, à propos* of the expulsion of the Anarchists from the Zurich Congress. [74]

An Anarchist is a man who—when he is not a police agent—is fated always and everywhere to attain the opposite of that which he attempts to achieve.

"To send working men to a Parliament," said Bordat, before the Lyons tribunal in 1893, "is to act like a mother who would take her daughter [138] to a brothel." Thus it is also in the name of *morality* that the Anarchists repudiate political action. But what is the outcome of their fear of parliamentary corruption? The glorification of theft, ("Put money in thy purse," wrote Most in his *Freiheit*, already in 1880), the exploits of the Duvals and Ravachols, who in the name of the "cause" commit the most vulgar and disgusting crimes. The Russian writer, *Herzen*, relates somewhere how on arriving at some small Italian town, he met only priests and bandits, and was greatly perplexed, being unable to decide which were the priests and which the bandits. And this is the position of every impartial person to-day; for how are you going to divine where the "companion" ends and the bandit begins? The Anarchists themselves are not always sure, as was proved by the controversy caused in their ranks by the Ravachol affair. Thus the better among them, those whose honesty is absolutely unquestionable, constantly fluctuate in their views of the "propaganda of deed.

"Condemn the propaganda of deed?" says Elysée Reclus. "But what is this propaganda except the preaching of well-doing and love of humanity by example? Those who call the "propaganda of deed" acts of violence prove that they have not understood the meaning of this expression. The Anarchist who understands his part, instead of massacring somebody or other, will exclusively strive to bring this person round to his opinions, and to make of him an adept who, in his turn, will make "propaganda [139] of deed" by showing himself good and just to all those whom he may meet." [75]

We will not ask what is left of the Anarchist who has divorced himself from the tactics of "deeds."

We only ask the reader to consider the following lines: "The editor of the *Sempre Avanti* wrote to Elysée Reclus asking him for his true opinion of Ravachol. 'I admire his courage, his goodness of heart, his greatness of soul, the generosity with which he pardons his enemies, or rather his betrayers. I hardly know of any men who have surpassed him in nobleness of conduct. I reserve the question as to how far it is always desirable to push to extremities one's own right, and whether other considerations moved by a spirit of human solidarity ought not to prevail. Still I am none the less one of those who recognise in Ravachol a hero of a magnanimity but little common.'" [76]

This does not at all fit in with the declaration quoted above, and it proves irrefutably that citizen Reclus fluctuates, that he does not know exactly where his "companion" ends and the bandit begins. The problem is the more difficult to solve that there are a good many individuals who are at the same time "bandits" and Anarchists. Ravachol was no exception. At the [140] house of the Anarchists, Oritz and Chiericotti, recently arrested at Paris, an enormous mass of stolen goods were found. Nor is it only in France that you have the combination of these two apparently different trades. It will suffice to remind the reader of the Austrians Kammerer and Stellmacher.

Kropotkine would have us believe that Anarchist morality, a morality free from all obligations or sanction, opposed to all utilitarian calculations, is the same as the natural morality of the people, "the morality from the habit of well doing." [77] The morality of the Anarchists is that of persons who look upon all human action from the abstract point of view of the unlimited rights of the individual, and who, in the name of these rights, pass a verdict of "Not guilty" on the most atrocious deeds, the most revolting arbitrary acts. "What matter the victims," exclaimed the Anarchist poet Laurent Tailhade, on the very evening of Vaillant's outrage, at the banquet of the "Plume" Society, "provided the gesture is beautiful?"

Tailhade is a decadent, who, because he is *blasé* has the courage of his Anarchist opinions. In fact the Anarchists combat democracy because democracy, according to them, is nothing but the tyranny of the majority as against the minority. The majority has no right to impose its wishes upon the minority. But if this is so, in the name [141] of what moral principle do the Anarchists revolt against the bourgeoisie? Because the bourgeoisie are not a minority? Or because they do not do what they "will" to do?

"Do as thou would'st," proclaim the Anarchists. The bourgeoisie "want" to exploit the proletariat, and do it remarkably well. They thus follow the Anarchist precept, and the "companions" are very wrong to complain of their conduct. They become altogether ridiculous when they combat the bourgeoisie in the name of their victims. "What matters the death of vague human beings"—continues the Anarchist logician Tailhade—"if thereby the individual affirms himself?" Here we have the true morality of the Anarchists; it is also that of the crowned heads. *Sic volo, sic jubeo!* [78]

Thus, in the name of the revolution, the Anarchists serve the cause of reaction; in the name of morality they approve the most immoral acts; in the name of individual liberty they trample under foot all the rights of their fellows.

And this is why the whole Anarchist doctrine founders upon its own logic. If any maniac may, because he "wants" to, kill as many men as he likes, society, composed of an immense [142] number of individuals, may certainly bring him to his senses, not because it is its caprice, but because it is its duty, because such is the *conditio sine quâ non* of its existence.

FOOTNOTES:

[64] In their dreams of riots and even of the Revolution, the Anarchists, burn, with real passion and delight, all title-deeds of property, and all governmental documents. It is Kropotkine especially who attributes immense importance to these *auto-da-fe*. Really, one would think him a rebellious civil servant.

[65] Republished in the *Peuple* of Lyons, December 20, 1893.

[66] "Anarchist Communism," p. 8.

[67] Kropotkine's preface to the Russian edition of Bakounine's pamphlet "La Commune de Paris et la notion de l'Etat." Geneva, 1892, p. 5.

[68] Ibid., same page.

[69] J. Grave "La Société Mourante et L'Anarchie," p. 253.

[70] Ibid., p. 249.

[71] Ibid., pp. 250-251.

[72] *Vorwärts*, January 23, 1894.

[73] "The companions were looking for someone to advance funds, but infamous capital did not seem in a hurry to reply to their appeal. I urged on infamous capital, and succeeded in persuading it that it was to its own interest to facilitate the publication of an Anarchist paper. But don't imagine that I with frank brutality offered the Anarchists the encouragement of the Prefect of police. I sent a well-dressed bourgeois to one of the most active and intelligent of them. He explained that having made a fortune in the druggist line, he wanted to devote a part of his income to advancing the Socialist propaganda. This bourgeois, anxious to be devoured, inspired the companions with no suspicion. Through his hands I placed the caution-money" [caution-money has to be deposited before starting a paper in France] "in the coffers of the State, and

the journal, *La Révolution Sociale*, made its appearance. It was a weekly paper, my druggist's generosity not extending to the expenses of a daily."—"Souvenirs d'un Préfet de Police." "Memoirs of a Prefect of Police." By J. Andrieux. (Jules Rouff et Cie, Paris, 1885.) Vol. I., p. 337, etc.

[74] In passing, we may remark that it is in the name of freedom of speech that the Anarchists claim to be admitted to Socialist Congresses. Yet this is the opinion of the French official journal of the Anarchists upon these Congresses:—"The Anarchists may congratulate themselves that some of their number attended the Troyes Congress. Absurd, motiveless, and senseless as an Anarchist Congress would be, just as logical is it to take advantage of Socialist Congresses in order to develop our ideas there."—*La Révolte*, 6-12 January, 1889. May not we also, in the name of freedom, ask the "companions" to leave us alone?

[75] See in the *L'Etudiant Socialiste* of Brussels, No. 6 (1894) the republication of the declaration made by Elysée Reclus, to a "correspondent" who had questioned him upon the Anarchist attempts.

[76] The *Twentieth Century*, a weekly Radical magazine, New York, September, 1892, p. 15.

[77] See Kropotkine's *Anarchist Communism*, pp. 34-35; also his *Anarchie dans l'Evolution Socialiste*, pp. 24-25, and many passages in his *Morale Anarchiste*.

[78] The papers have just announced that Tailhade was wounded by an explosion at the Restaurant Foyot. The telegram (*La Tribune de Genève*, 5th April, 1894) adds—"M. Tailhade is constantly protesting against the Anarchist theories he is credited with. One of the house surgeons, having reminded him of his article and the famous phrase quoted above, M. Tailhade remained silent, and asked for chloral to alleviate his pain."

[143]

CHAPTER IX—CONCLUSION

THE BOURGEOISIE, ANARCHISM, AND SOCIALISM

The "father of Anarchy," the "immortal" Proudhon, bitterly mocked at those people for whom the revolution consisted of acts of violence, the exchange of blows, the shedding of blood. The descendants of the "father," the modern Anarchists, understand by revolution only this brutally childish method. Everything that is not violence is a betrayal of the cause, a foul compromise with "authority." [79] The scared bourgeoisie does not know what to do against them. In the domain of theory they are absolutely impotent with regard to the Anarchists, who are their own *enfants terribles*. The bourgeoisie was the first to propagate the theory of *laissez faire*, of dishevelled individualism. Their most eminent philosopher of to-day, Herbert Spencer, is nothing but a conservative Anarchist. The "companions" are active and zealous persons, who carry the bourgeois reasoning to its logical conclusion.

[144]

The magistrates of the French bourgeois Republic have condemned Grave to prison, and his book, "La Société Mourante et l'Anarchie" to destruction. The bourgeois men of letters declare this puerile book a profound work, and its author a man of rare intellect.

And not only has the bourgeoisie [80] no theoretical weapons with which to combat the Anarchists; they see their young folk enamoured of the Anarchist doctrine. In this society, satiated and rotten to the marrow of its bones, where all faiths are long since dead, where all sincere opinions appear ridiculous, in this *monde où l'on s'ennui*, where after having exhausted all forms of enjoyment they no longer know in what new fancy, in what fresh excess to seek novel sensations, there are people who lend a willing ear to the song of the Anarchist siren. Amongst the Paris "companions" there are already not a few men quite *comme il faut*, men about town who, as the French writer, Raoul Allier, says, wear nothing less than patent leather shoes, and put a green carnation in their button-holes before they go to meetings. Decadent writers and artists are converted to Anarchism and propagate its theories in reviews like the *Mercure de France*, [145] *La Plume*, etc. And this is comprehensible enough. One might wonder indeed if Anarchism, an essentially bourgeois doctrine, had not found adepts among the French bourgeoisie, the most *blasée* of all bourgeoisies.

By taking possession of the Anarchist doctrine, the decadent, *fin-de-siècle* writers restore to it its true character of bourgeois individualism. If Kropotkine and Reclus speak in the name of the worker, oppressed by the capitalist, *La Plume* and the *Mercure de France* speak in the name of the *individual* who is seeking to shake off all the trammels of society in order that he may at last do freely what he "wants" to. Thus Anarchism comes back to its starting-point. Stirner said: "Nothing for me goes beyond myself." Laurent Tailhade says: "What matters the death of vague human beings, if thereby the individual affirms himself."

The bourgeoisie no longer knows where to turn. "I who have fought so much for Positivism," moans Emile Zola, "well, yes! after thirty years of this struggle, I feel my convictions are shaken. Religious faith would have prevented such theories from being propagated; but has it not almost disappeared to-day? Who will give us a new ideal?"

Alas, gentlemen, there is no ideal for walking corpses such as you! You will try everything. You will become Buddhists, Druids, Sârs, Chaldeans, Occultists, Magi, Theosophists, or Anarchists, whichever you prefer—and yet you will remain what you are now—beings without faith [146] or principle, bags, emptied by history. The ideal of the bourgeois has lived.

For ourselves, Social-Democrats, we have nothing to fear from the Anarchist propaganda. The child of the bourgeoisie, Anarchism, will never have any serious influence upon the proletariat. If among the Anarchists there are workmen who sincerely desire the good of their class, and who sacrifice themselves to what they believe to be the good cause, it is only thanks to a misunderstanding that they find themselves in this camp. They only know the struggle for the emancipation of the proletariat under the form which the Anarchists are trying to give it. When more enlightened they will come to us.

Here is an example to prove this. During the trial of the Anarchists at Lyons in 1883, the working man Desgranges related how he had become an Anarchist, he who had formerly taken part in the political movement, and had even been elected a municipal councillor at Villefranche in November, 1879. "In 1881, in the month of September, when the dyers' strike broke out at Villefranche, I was elected secretary of the strike committee, and it was during this memorable event . that I became convinced of the necessity of suppressing authority, for authority spells despotism. During this strike, when the employers refused to discuss the matter with the workers, what did the prefectural and communal administrations do to settle the dispute? Fifty gendarmes, with sword in hand, were told off to settle the question. That is what is called the pacific means employed by [147] Governments. It was then, at the end of this strike, that some working men, myself among the number, understood the necessity of seriously studying economic questions, and, in order to do so, we agreed to meet in the evening to study together." [81] It is hardly necessary to add that this group became Anarchist.

That is how the trick is done. A working man, active and intelligent, supports the programme of one or the other bourgeois party. The bourgeois talk about the well-being of the people, the workers, but betray them on the first opportunity. The working man who has believed in the sincerity of these persons is indignant, wants to separate from them, and decides to study seriously "economic questions." An Anarchist comes along, and reminding him of the treachery of the bourgeois, and the sabres of the gendarmes, assures him that the political struggle is nothing but bourgeois nonsense, and that in order to emancipate the workers political action must be given up, making the destruction of the State the final aim. The working man who was only beginning to study the situation thinks the "companion" is right, and so he becomes a convinced and devoted Anarchist! What would happen, if pursuing his studies of the social question further, he had understood that the "companion" was a pretentious ignoramus, that he talked twaddle, that his "Ideal" is a delusion and a snare, that [148] outside bourgeois politics there is, opposed to these, the political action of the proletariat, which will put an end to the very existence of capitalist society? He would have become a Social-Democrat.

Thus the more widely our ideas become known among the working classes, and they are thus becoming more and more widely known, the less will proletarians be inclined to follow the Anarchist. Anarchism, with the exception of its "learned" housebreakers, will more and more transform itself into a kind of bourgeois sport, for the purpose of providing sensations for "individuals" who have indulged too freely in the pleasures of the world, the flesh and the devil.

And when the proletariat are masters of the situation, they will only need to look at the "companions," and even the "finest" of them will be silenced; they will only have to breathe to disperse all the Anarchist dust to the winds of heaven.

FOOTNOTES:

[79] It is true that men like Reclus do not always approve of such notions of the revolution. But again we ask, what is left of the Anarchist when once he rejects the "propaganda of deed"? A sentimental, visionary bourgeois—nothing more.

[80] In order to obtain some idea of the weakness of the bourgeois theorists and politicians in their struggle against the Anarchists, it suffices to read the articles of C. Lombroso and A. Bérard in the *Revue des Revues*, 15th February, 1894, or the article of J. Bourdeau in the *Revue de Paris*, 15th March, 1894. The latter can only appeal to "human nature" which, he thinks, "will not be changed through the pamphlets of Kropotkine and the bombs of Ravachol."

[81] See report of the Anarchist trial before the Correctional Police and the Court of Appeal of Lyons; Lyons, 1883, pp. 90-91.

***